100 DEVOTIONS

*for coloring &
creative journaling*

Inspire®

Worship

Tyndale House Publishers
Carol Stream, Illinois

Visit Tyndale online at tyndale.com and inspirebible.com.

Tyndale, Tyndale's quill logo, *New Living Translation*, *NLT*, and *Inspire* are registered trademarks of Tyndale House Ministries.

Inspire Worship copyright © 2022 by Robert K. Brown and Mark R. Norton. All rights reserved.

Compiled and Edited by Robert K. Brown and Mark R. Norton

Hymn stories by William J. Petersen and Randy Peterson

Interior design and typesetting by Peachtree Publishing Services

Cover design by Nicole Grimes

ISBN 978-1-4964-6796-6

Printed in China

28 27 26 25 24 23 22
7 6 5 4 3 2 1

Contents

PREFACE

"Shout with joy to the Lord, all the earth! Worship the Lord with gladness. Come before him, singing with joy."
Psalm 100:1-2

From the earliest days of Christian faith, singing hymns has been an essential part of worship. In the book of Acts we find Paul and Silas "praying and singing hymns to God" (Acts 16:25) while chained in the Philippian jail. It was also the apostle Paul who encouraged believers with these words: "Be filled with the Holy Spirit, singing psalms and hymns and spiritual songs among yourselves, and making music to the Lord in your hearts" (Ephesians 5:18-19).

But the tradition of singing in worship is far older than even Paul and the early Christians. Many centuries earlier, Moses and his sister, Miriam, led the nation of Israel in song after their miraculous escape through the Red Sea. And who can forget King David, who composed numerous psalms expressing both personal and corporate praise. Centuries later, translations of David's psalms would provide the inspiration for many of our English hymns and choruses.

You are opening the door to a sacred space. Relax, reflect, and connect to God through creative expression. Let this beautifully designed collection of one hundred great hymns strengthen your faith as you quietly meditate on their rich words and imagery. And don't forget to hum along as you embellish the artwork! Allow each reading to encourage you to stand strong, lean on God's grace, and rest in knowing that he has a wonderful purpose for your life. As you actively worship through this treasury of hymns, look forward to the day when all believers—past, present, and future—will join in one great chorus around God's throne. For as hymnwriter Isaac Watts once recognized, "The singing of God's praise is the part of worship most closely related to heaven."

ABIDE WITH ME

Abide with me; fast falls the eventide;
The darkness deepens; LORD, with me abide!
When other helpers fail and comforts flee,
Help of the helpless, O abide with me.

I fear no foe, with Thee at hand to bless;
Ills have no weight, and tears no bitterness.
Where is death's sting? Where, grave, thy victory?
I triumph still, if Thou abide with me.

Hold Thou Thy cross before my closing eyes;
Shine through the gloom and point me to the skies;
Heaven's morning breaks, and earth's vain shadows flee;
In life, in death, O LORD, abide with me.

HENRY FRANCIS LYTE (1793–1847)

HENRY LYTE coined the phrase, "It is better to wear out than to rust out." And Henry Lyte wore out when he was fifty-four years old, an obscure pastor who labored for twenty-three years in a poor church in a fishing village in Devonshire, England. This hymn, written shortly before his death, was inspired by the words of the two disciples met by Jesus on the road to Emmaus: "Stay the night with us, since it is getting late" (Luke 24:29).

As Lyte wrote this, he knew he was dying of tuberculosis and asthma. It was "eventide" for him, darkness was deepening, and he felt very much alone. But he was not alone, and we are not alone even in our darkest times. Our Lord is with us, "the help of the helpless," the one who never changes, our guide and security. He will never leave us nor forsake us.

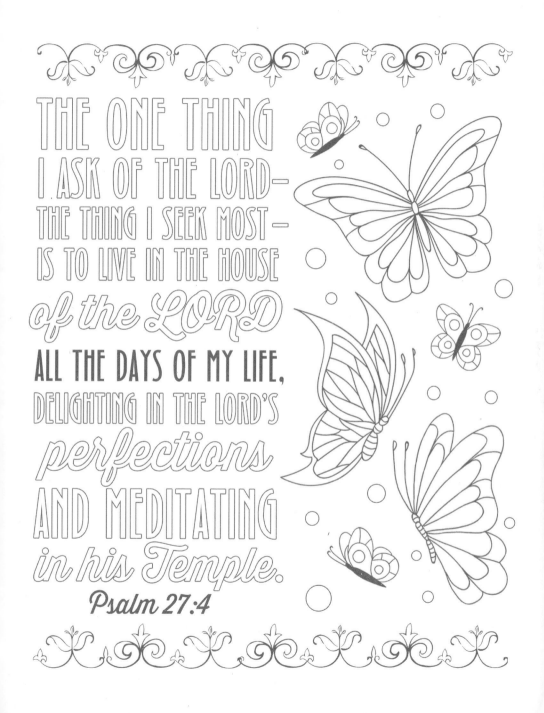

THE ONE THING I ASK OF THE LORD—THE THING I SEEK MOST—IS TO LIVE IN THE HOUSE *of the LORD* ALL THE DAYS OF MY LIFE, DELIGHTING IN THE LORD'S *perfections* AND MEDITATING *in his Temple.*

Psalm 27:4

Alas! And Did My Savior Bleed?

He was pierced for our rebellion, crushed for our sins. He was beaten so we could be whole. He was whipped so we could be healed. All of us, like sheep, have strayed away. We have left God's paths to follow our own. Yet the LORD laid on him the sins of us all.

Isaiah 53:5-6

Alas! and did my Savior bleed
And did my Sovereign die?
Would He devote that sacred head
For sinners such as I?

Was it for sins that I have done
He suffered on the tree?
Amazing pity! grace unknown!
And love beyond degree!

Well might the sun in darkness hide
And shut His glories in,
When Christ, the great Redeemer, died
For man the creature's sin.

Thus might I hide my blushing face
While His dear cross appears,
Dissolve my heart in thankfulness,
And melt mine eyes to tears.

But drops of grief can ne'er repay
The debt of love I owe;
Here, Lord, I give myself away—
'Tis all that I can do.

ISAAC WATTS (1674–1748)

WE NEVER KNOW how deeply our actions affect the lives of others. This hymn by Isaac Watts has certainly touched the hearts of millions through the centuries. After drawing the stark contrasts between the sacrificial death of the mighty Maker and the unworthiness of the sinful creature, he concludes with the consecration, "Here, Lord, I give myself away—'tis all that I can do."

All Creatures of Our God and King

Praise the LORD from the earth, you creatures of the ocean depths, fire and hail, snow and clouds, wind and weather that obey him, mountains and all hills, fruit trees and all cedars, wild animals and all livestock, small scurrying animals and birds, kings of the earth and all people, rulers and judges of the earth, young men and young women, old men and children. Let them all praise the name of the LORD.

Psalm 148:7-13

All creatures of our God and King,
Lift up your voice and with us sing
Alleluia! Alleluia!
Thou burning sun with golden beam,
Thou silver moon with softer gleam!

O praise Him, O praise Him!
Alleluia! Alleluia! Alleluia!

Let all things their Creator bless,
And worship Him in humbleness,
O praise Him! Alleluia!
Praise, praise the Father, praise the Son,
And praise the Spirit, Three in One!

FRANCIS OF ASSISI (1182–1226)
TRANSLATED BY WILLIAM H. DRAPER (1855–1933)

SAINT FRANCIS OF ASSISI is perhaps best known as a nature lover. You may recall the painting in which the Italian artist Giotto depicts him feeding the birds. One writer spoke of him this way: "With smiles he met the friendless, fed the poor, freed a trapped bird, led home a child. Although he spoke no word, his text, God's love, the town did not forget."

A soldier in his early years, Francis resolved to imitate the life of Christ, denounced his wealth, and founded the Franciscan Order of Friars. He wrote sixty hymns of praise and worship and encouraged church music in every way he could.

All Hail the Power of Jesus' Name

On his robe at his thigh
was written this title:
King of all kings and
Lord of all lords.

Revelation 19:16

All hail the pow'r of Jesus' name!
Let angels prostrate fall;
Bring forth the royal diadem,
And crown Him Lord of all;
Bring forth the royal diadem,
And crown Him Lord of all!

O that with yonder sacred throng
We at His feet may fall!
We'll join the everlasting song,
And crown Him Lord of all;
We'll join the everlasting song,
And crown Him Lord of all!

EDWARD PERRONET (1726–1792)
ALTERED BY JOHN RIPPON (1751–1836)

EDWARD PERRONET was not an easy person to get along with. After being a minister in the Anglican Church for some time, he became fed up with what he felt was the church's "nonsense" and became a Methodist, joining up with the Wesleys.

Perronet soon broke with the Wesleys over the issue of who could administer the sacraments. He joined a group called the Connexion but later broke with them as well. It was as a minister of an independent church in Canterbury that he wrote this majestic hymn.

ON HIS ROBE
AT HIS THIGH
was written this title:
King of all kings
and
Lord of all lords.
Revelation 19:16

All the Way My Savior Leads Me

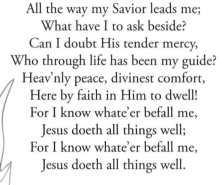

All the way my Savior leads me;
  What have I to ask beside?
Can I doubt His tender mercy,
  Who through life has been my guide?
Heav'nly peace, divinest comfort,
  Here by faith in Him to dwell!
For I know whate'er befall me,
  Jesus doeth all things well;
For I know whate'er befall me,
  Jesus doeth all things well.

All the way my Savior leads me;
  Oh, the fullness of His love!
Perfect rest to me is promised
  In my Father's house above:
When my spirit, cloth'd immortal,
  Wings its flight to realms of day,
This my song through endless ages:
  Jesus led me all the way;
This my song through endless ages:
  Jesus led me all the way.

FANNY JANE CROSBY (1820–1915)

"JESUS DOETH all things well." It probably wasn't always easy for Fanny Crosby to believe that. When she was only six weeks old, she lost her sight because of a doctor's error.

This particular hymn was written on a day when Crosby needed five dollars and didn't know where she would get it. She prayed about it, and a few minutes later a stranger came to her door and handed her that exact amount.

She was amazed at the Lord's marvelous answer to her simple prayer. She wrote, "My first thought was, 'It is so wonderful the way the Lord leads me.'"

All Things Bright and Beautiful

All things bright and beautiful,
All creatures great and small,
And all things wise and wonderful;
The Lord God made them all.

Each little flow'r that opens up,
Each little bird that sings,
He made their glowing colors and
He made their tiny wings.

The purple-headed mountain,
The river running by,
The sunset and the morning light
That brightens up the sky.

The cold wind in the wintertime,
The pleasant summer sun,
The ripe fruits in the garden now,
He made them ev'ry one.

He gave us eyes to see them all,
And lips that we might tell
How great is the Almighty God
Who has made all things well.

Cecil Frances Alexander (1818–1895)

CECIL ALEXANDER and her husband, William, a parish minister in Londonderry, Ireland, served in a rural area. She visited the poor families and gathered the children around her for instruction in the Bible, the catechism, and the Apostles' Creed.

Often when we think of God the Creator, we consider the vast galaxies of space and the mighty billowing oceans, but this hymn, written for boys and girls, talks of little flowers with glowing colors, little birds with tiny wings, purple-headed mountains, ripe fruits in the garden, and meadows where we play.

IN THE BEGINNING THE Word ALREADY EXISTED. JOHN 1:1

Amazing Grace

God saved you by his grace when you believed. And you can't take credit for this; it is a gift from God. Salvation is not a reward for the good things we have done, so none of us can boast about it.

Ephesians 2:8-9

Amazing grace! how sweet the sound—
That saved a wretch like me!
I once was lost but now am found,
Was blind but now I see.

'Twas grace that taught my heart to fear,
And grace my fears relieved;
How precious did that grace appear
The hour I first believed!

The Lord has promised good to me,
His word my hope secures;
He will my shield and portion be
As long as life endures.

Through many dangers, toils and snares
I have already come;
'Tis grace hath brought me safe thus far,
And grace will lead me home.

When we've been there ten thousand years,
Bright shining as the sun,
We've no less days to sing God's praise
Than when we'd first begun.

JOHN NEWTON (1725–1807)
STANZA 5 BY JOHN P. REES (1828–1900)

THE GIFT OF FORGIVENESS is often best appreciated by those who need it the most. The Reverend John Newton experienced this truth firsthand. His tombstone tells the story: "John Newton, clerk, once an infidel and Libertine, a servant of slavers in Africa, was, by the rich mercy of our Lord and Savior Jesus Christ, preserved, restored, pardoned, and appointed to preach the faith he had so long labored to destroy." These words were written by Newton himself, a testimony to God's transforming power.

GOD SAVED YOU BY HIS GRACE when you BELIEVED.

Ephesians 2:8

A Mighty Fortress Is Our God

A mighty fortress is our God, a bulwark never failing;
Our helper He amid the flood of mortal ills prevailing.
For still our ancient foe doth seek to work us woe—
His craft and pow'r are great, and, armed with cruel hate,
On earth is not his equal.

Did we in our own strength confide, our striving would be losing,
Were not the right man on our side, the man of God's own choosing.
Dost ask who that may be? Christ Jesus, it is He—
Lord Sabaoth His name, from age to age the same,
And He must win the battle.

And though this world, with devils filled, should threaten to undo us,
We will not fear, for God hath willed His truth to triumph through us.
The prince of darkness grim, we tremble not for him—
His rage we can endure, for lo! his doom is sure:
One little word shall fell him.

That word above all earthly pow'rs, no thanks to them, abideth;
The Spirit and the gifts are ours through Him who with us sideth.
Let goods and kindred go, this mortal life also—
The body they may kill; God's truth abideth still:
His kingdom is forever.

MARTIN LUTHER (1483–1546)
TRANSLATED BY FREDERICK H. HEDGE (1805–1890)

AFTER POSTING his Ninety-Five Theses on the door of Wittenberg's Castle Church in October 1517, Martin Luther faced many years of trials and persecution. And during the years of the ensuing Protestant Reformation, Luther came to know better than most the gracious power of God's sheltering hand.

In the comforting words of Psalm 46, Luther found the inspiration for this hymn that would become the battle cry of the Protestant Reformation. Many who suffered for their faith during that time found solid comfort in Luther's words of faith and praise.

And Can It Be?

So now there is no condemnation for those who belong to Christ Jesus. . . . [God] sent his own Son in a body like the bodies we sinners have. And in that body God declared an end to sin's control over us by giving his Son as a sacrifice for our sins.

Romans 8:1, 3

And can it be that I should gain
An interest in the Savior's blood?
Died He for me, who caused His pain?
For me, who Him to death pursued?

Amazing love! how can it be
That Thou, my Lord, shouldst die for me?

He left His Father's throne above,
So free, so infinite His grace!
Emptied Himself of all but love,
And bled for Adam's helpless race!
'Tis mercy all, immense and free,
For, O my God, it found out me.

No condemnation now I dread;
Jesus, and all in Him is mine;
Alive in Him, my living Head,
And clothed in righteousness divine,
Bold I approach th' eternal throne,
And claim the crown, through Christ my own.

CHARLES WESLEY (1707–1788)

CHARLES WESLEY is probably the greatest hymn writer the church has ever known. From the time of his conversion in 1738, Wesley wrote an average of two hymns a week every week for fifty years, composing between five and six thousand hymns during his lifetime. Most of these hymns were written on horseback as he traveled with his brother John, preaching and ministering to the poor.

20

So now there is
no condemnation
for those
WHO BELONG
TO CHRIST JESUS.
Romans 8:1

Beneath the Cross of Jesus

When Jesus had tasted it, he said, "It is finished!" Then he bowed his head and gave up his spirit.

John 19:30

Beneath the cross of Jesus
I fain would take my stand—
The shadow of a mighty Rock
Within a weary land;
A home within the wilderness,
A rest upon the way,
From the burning of the noontide heat,
And the burden of the day.

ELIZABETH CECELIA CLEPHANE (1830–1869)

ELIZABETH CECELIA CLEPHANE spent her whole life in Scotland. Daughter of a county sheriff, she grew up in the village of Melrose. She suffered from poor health most of her life, but that didn't keep her from serving others. She regularly helped the poor and those with disabilities, even selling a horse and carriage to give more money. Her cheery attitude and selfless spirit earned her the nickname, "The Sunbeam of Melrose." She wrote eight hymns, including "The Ninety and Nine."

THEN HE BOWED
HIS HEAD
AND GAVE UP
HIS SPIRIT.
JOHN 19:30

BE STILL, MY SOUL

Be still, my soul! the Lord is on thy side;
Bear patiently the cross of grief or pain;
Leave to thy God to order and provide;
In every change He faithful will remain.
Be still, my soul! thy best, thy heavenly Friend
Through thorny ways leads to a joyful end.

KATHARINA AMALIA VON SCHLEGEL (1697–?)
TRANSLATED BY JANE LAURIE BORTHWICK (1813–1897)

IN THE MIDST of the psalmist's troubles, the Lord said, "Be still, and know that I am God." These words spoke to Katharina von Schlegel in the turbulent times of post-Reformation Germany. A century after Luther's reforms, central Europe was racked by the Thirty Years' War, which pitted Catholics against Protestants. The Lutheran church lapsed into formalism and dead orthodoxy. In the darkness of that time, God raised up the Pietist movement, which stressed personal holiness, charity, missions, and music.

Today's hymn, penned by the leading woman of the Pietist movement, a canoness of a women's seminary, was among those forgotten songs.

BLESSED ASSURANCE

We can boldly enter
heaven's Most Holy
Place because of the
blood of Jesus. By his
death, Jesus opened a
new and life-giving way
through the curtain into
the Most Holy Place.

Hebrews 10:19-20

Blessed assurance, Jesus is mine!
O what a foretaste of glory divine!
Heir of salvation, purchase of God,
Born of His Spirit, washed in His blood.

This is my story, this is my song,
Praising my Savior all the day long;
This is my story, this is my song,
Praising my Savior all the day long.

FANNY JANE CROSBY (1820–1915)

FANNY CROSBY wrote more than eight thousand hymns and used more than two hundred pen names. The fact that she was blind didn't diminish her productivity.

Phoebe Palmer Knapp, wife of the founder of Metropolitan Life Insurance Company, composed a tune in 1873 and brought it to Crosby in Brooklyn. "Play it for me on the organ," Crosby asked. Knapp did and then asked, "What does this tune say?" She turned to see Crosby kneeling in prayer. Knapp played it a second time and then a third. Then the blind woman responded, "That says, 'Blessed assurance, Jesus is mine! O what a foretaste of glory divine!'"

Blest Be the Tie That Binds

Make every effort to keep yourselves united in the Spirit, binding yourselves together with peace. For there is one body and one Spirit, just as you have been called to one glorious hope for the future. There is one Lord, one faith, one baptism, one God and Father.

Ephesians 4:3-6

Blest be the tie that binds
Our hearts in Christian love:
The fellowship of kindred minds
Is like to that above.

When we asunder part,
It gives us inward pain;
But we shall still be joined in heart,
And hope to meet again.

JOHN FAWCETT (1740–1817)

ORPHANED when he was twelve, then forced to work fourteen hours a day in a sweatshop, John Fawcett learned to read by candlelight. He began his ministry at a poor church in Wainsgate in northern England.

After seven years of ministry, Fawcett received a call to the prestigious Carter's Lane Church in London. But as he was saying his farewells and saw the tears on the faces of his people, he changed his mind and decided to stay.

Not long afterward, he wrote this hymn for the congregation at Wainsgate. He recognized that the bond of love he knew there was worth more than any material wealth.

MAKE EVERY
effort
TO KEEP
YOURSELVES
UNITED IN THE
Spirit,
BINDING
YOURSELVES
TOGETHER WITH PEACE.
EPHESIANS 4:3

Breathe on Me, Breath of God

Breathe on me, Breath of God,
Fill me with life anew,
That I may love what Thou dost love,
And do what Thou wouldst do.

Breathe on me, Breath of God,
Until my heart is pure,
Until with Thee I will one will,
To do and to endure.

Breathe on me, Breath of God,
So shall I never die,
But live with Thee the perfect life
Of Thine eternity.

EDWIN HATCH (1835–1889)

EDWIN HATCH was a learned man who could string together sentences filled with many-syllable words. After all, he was a distinguished lecturer in ecclesiastical history at Oxford and a professor of classics at Trinity College in Quebec.

But when it came to expressing his faith, Hatch was "as simple and unaffected as a child." This hymn is filled with one-syllable words and is a simple, heartfelt prayer.

The Spirit of God, who raised Jesus from the dead, lives in you.

ROMANS 8:11

Cleanse Me

Search me, O God, and know my heart today;
Try me, O Savior, know my thoughts, I pray.
See if there be some wicked way in me;
Cleanse me from every sin, and set me free.

O Holy Ghost, revival comes from Thee;
Send a revival, start the work in me.
Thy Word declares Thou wilt supply our need;
For blessings now, O Lord, I humbly plead.

JAMES EDWIN ORR (1912–1987)

IN 1936, at the age of twenty-four, evangelist J. Edwin Orr wrote this hymn during an Easter evangelistic campaign in New Zealand.

As Orr was about to leave New Zealand, four Maori girls came and sang him their native song of farewell. Impressed by the tune and still stirred by the revival he had witnessed, Orr quickly scribbled the stanzas of this hymn on the back of an envelope as he waited in the post office of Ngaruawahia, New Zealand.

32

POINT OUT ANYTHING IN ME THAT OFFENDS YOU, AND LEAD ME ALONG THE PATH OF EVERLASTING LIFE.
PSALM 139:24

Come, Thou Almighty King

Come, let us sing to the LORD! Let us shout joyfully to the Rock of our salvation. Let us come to him with thanksgiving. Let us sing psalms of praise to him. For the LORD is a great God, a great King above all gods.

Psalm 95:1-3

Come, Thou Almighty King,
Help us Thy name to sing,
Help us to praise:
Father! all-glorious,
O'er all victorious,
Come, and reign over us,
Ancient of Days.

To Thee, great One in Three,
Eternal praises be,
Hence evermore;
Thy sov'reign majesty
May we in glory see,
And to eternity
Love and adore.

AUTHOR UNKNOWN

THIS hymn appeared anonymously in George Whitefield's hymnbook, published in 1757. It is usually attributed to Charles Wesley, but was probably published anonymously for a good reason. Scholars think Wesley wrote this hymn as an imitation of the English national anthem, "God Save Our Gracious King." The national anthem had just been written, and it had become popular throughout England. This hymn may have been Wesley's way of keeping priorities straight.

COME, THOU FOUNT OF EVERY BLESSING

Come, Thou Fount of ev'ry blessing,
Tune my heart to sing Thy grace;
Streams of mercy never ceasing,
Call for songs of loudest praise:
Teach me some melodious sonnet,
Sung by flaming tongues above;
Praise the mount—O fix me on it,
Mount of God's unchanging love.

Here I raise mine Ebenezer;
Hither by Thy help I'm come;
And I hope, by Thy good pleasure,
Safely to arrive at home:
Jesus sought me when a stranger,
Wand'ring from the fold of God;
He, to save my soul from danger,
Interposed His precious blood.

ROBERT ROBINSON (1735–1790)

ROBERT ROBINSON had always been prone to wander. Apprenticed to a barber at fourteen, he spent more time reading and playing with friends than cutting hair. Then, still a teen, he went to a George Whitefield meeting, intending to ridicule it—and instead was converted. After his apprenticeship was over, Robinson went into the ministry. He wrote this hymn at the age of twenty-three as he served at the Calvinistic Methodist Church in Norfolk, England.

Late in life, Robinson did stray from the faith. Once, in a stagecoach, he sat by a lady who was reading a hymnbook. She showed him "Come, Thou Fount," saying how wonderful it was. He tried to change the subject, but couldn't. Finally he said, "Madam, I am the unhappy man who wrote that hymn many years ago, and I would give a thousand worlds to enjoy the feelings I had then."

Come, Ye Sinners, Poor and Needy

When the teachers of religious law who were Pharisees saw him eating with tax collectors and other sinners, they asked his disciples, "Why does he eat with such scum?" When Jesus heard this, he told them, "Healthy people don't need a doctor—sick people do. I have come to call not those who think they are righteous, but those who know they are sinners."

Mark 2:16-17

Come, ye sinners, poor and needy,
Weak and wounded, sick and sore;
Jesus ready stands to save you,
Full of pity, love, and power;
He is able, He is able,
He is willing; doubt no more.

Come, ye weary, heavy laden,
Bruised and mangled by the Fall;
If you tarry till you're better,
You will never come at all;
Not the righteous, not the righteous;
Sinners Jesus came to call.

JOSEPH HART (1712–1768)

LONDON-BORN Joseph Hart struggled against God for years. Then he came under conviction. At times he was afraid to sleep, fearing he would "awake in hell." He went from church to church, but as he said, "everything served only to condemn me."

Finally at the age of forty-five he wandered into a Moravian chapel in London and heard words of hope. On returning home he knelt in prayer.

Three years later he became a minister and began writing hymns to touch the hearts of others who had experienced similar spiritual struggles.

Come, Ye Thankful People, Come

Come, ye thankful people, come,
Raise the song of harvest home;
All is safely gathered in,
Ere the winter storms begin;
God, our Maker, doth provide
For our wants to be supplied;
Come to God's own temple, come,
Raise the song of harvest home.

All the world is God's own field,
Fruit unto His praise to yield;
Wheat and tares together sown,
Unto joy or sorrow grown;
First the blade, and then the ear,
Then the full corn shall appear;
Lord of harvest, grant that we
Wholesome grain and pure may be.

HENRY ALFORD (1810–1871)

MANY CHRISTIANS are in the habit of giving thanks before meals. It is said that Henry Alford also gave thanks *after* meals, standing and offering his gratitude to God for the blessings just received. He also did this at the end of the day.

But this song isn't just about thanksgiving. It is also about work completed, a job well done. It is about aching muscles and full barns, sun-reddened faces and meals of plenty. It was written to be used at harvest festivals in villages throughout England. Each village observed a celebration whenever it brought in its harvest, and Alford, one of the leading churchmen in England in the nineteenth century, provided this hymn of thanks. It was originally called "After Harvest."

CROWN HIM WITH MANY CROWNS

Crown Him with many crowns,
The Lamb upon His throne;
Hark! how the heavenly anthem drowns
All music but its own.
Awake, my soul, and sing
Of Him who died for thee,
And hail Him as thy matchless King
Through all eternity.

Crown Him the Lord of life,
Who triumphed o'er the grave,
And rose victorious in the strife
For those He came to save;
His glories now we sing
Who died and rose on high,
Who died, eternal life to bring,
And lives, that death may die.

Crown Him the Lord of love;
Behold His hands and side,
Those wounds, yet visible above,
In beauty glorified.
All hail, Redeemer, hail!
For Thou hast died for me;
Thy praise and glory shall not fail
Throughout eternity.

MATTHEW BRIDGES (1800–1894)
GODFREY THRING (1823–1903)

MATTHEW BRIDGES became a convert to Roman Catholicism at the age of forty-eight and published this hymn three years later under the title "The Song of the Seraphs." Godfrey Thring, an Anglican clergyman, added several stanzas to the hymn about thirty years later, with Bridges's approval.

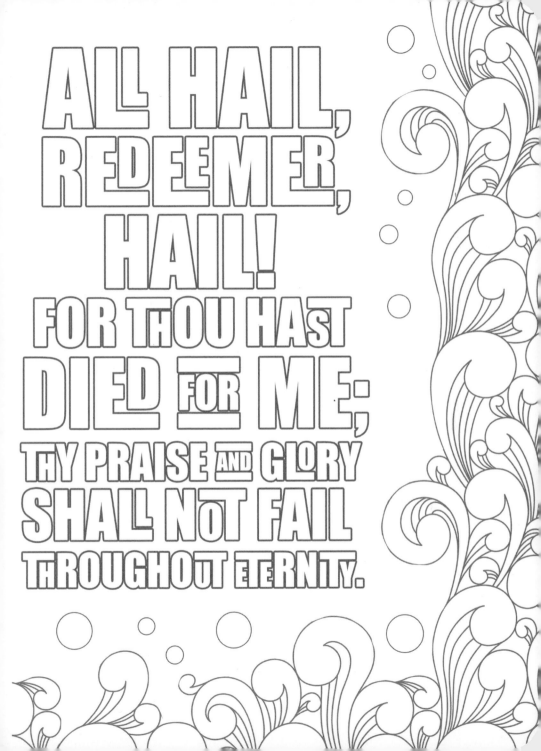

ALL HAIL, REDEEMER, HAIL! FOR THOU HAST DIED FOR ME; THY PRAISE AND GLORY SHALL NOT FAIL THROUGHOUT ETERNITY.

Day by Day and with Each Passing Moment

We are pressed on every side by troubles, but we are not crushed. We are perplexed, but not driven to despair. We are hunted down, but never abandoned by God. We get knocked down, but we are not destroyed.

2 Corinthians 4:8-9

Day by day and with each passing moment,
Strength I find to meet my trials here;
Trusting in my Father's wise bestowment,
I've no cause for worry or for fear.
He whose heart is kind beyond all measure
Gives unto each day what He deems best—
Lovingly, its part of pain and pleasure,
Mingling toil with peace and rest.

CAROLINA SANDELL BERG (1832–1903)
TRANSLATED BY ANDREW L. SKOOG (1856–1934)

GOD IS ALWAYS WITH US, even during our most painful experiences. Carolina Sandell Berg understood this truth personally. She was never strong as a child, so she spent much time in her father's study and grew especially close to him. When she was twenty-six, she accompanied her father, who was a parish pastor in Fröderyd, Sweden, on a voyage to Göteborg. As they stood on deck, the boat lurched and spilled Pastor Sandell overboard. The crew was unable to save him, and he drowned as his daughter looked on.

Berg was already well known for hymns she had published as a young girl, but this tragedy inspired many more. At the loss of her earthly father, she drew even closer to her heavenly Father. She discovered that even during the times of greatest loss, God's comforting presence was near.

We are hunted down,
BUT NEVER
abandoned
BY GOD.
2 Corinthians 4:9

Fairest Lord Jesus

Fairest Lord Jesus,
Ruler of all nature,
O Thou of God and man the son,
Thee will I cherish,
Thee will I honor,
Thou, my soul's glory, joy, and crown.

Fair are the meadows,
Fairer still the woodlands,
Robed in the blooming garb of spring:
Jesus is fairer,
Jesus is purer,
Who makes the woeful heart to sing.

Fair is the sunshine,
Fairer still the moonlight,
And all the twinkling starry host:
Jesus shines brighter,
Jesus shines purer,
Than all the angels heaven can boast.

MÜNSTER GESANGBUCH, 1677
TRANSLATOR UNKNOWN

THIS HYMN may have first been sung by followers of reformer John Hus, who lived near Prague around 1400. In an anti-Reformation purge, Hussites were expelled from Bohemia and went into Silesia, where they became weavers and cobblers, maintaining their faith in secret. But they had a strong tradition of hymn singing, and the most reliable tradition says that this hymn came from these humble Christians.

The hymn contains no comments on persecution, but only praise to a wonderful Savior. Whoever wrote the hymn was close to nature and adored God's creation, but recognized that even fairer than the creation is the Creator. This season as we bask in the beauties of all that God has given us to enjoy, we mustn't forget that Jesus is fairer and purer than all the blooming garb of spring.

FOR THE BEAUTY OF THE EARTH

For the beauty of the earth,
For the glory of the skies,
For the love which from our birth
Over and around us lies:

Lord of all, to Thee we raise
This our hymn of grateful praise.

For the beauty of each hour
Of the day and of the night,
Hill and vale, and tree and flower,
Sun and moon, and stars of light:

For the joy of ear and eye,
For the heart and mind's delight,
For the mystic harmony
Linking sense to sound and sight:

For Thyself, best Gift Divine!
To our race so freely given;
For that great, great love of Thine,
Peace on earth, and joy in heaven.

FOLLIOT SANFORD PIERPOINT (1835–1917)

FOLLIOT PIERPOINT was born in Bath but went away to attend Cambridge University, where he became a classical scholar and taught. But when he was twenty-nine years old, he returned to his hometown of Bath. The beauty of the countryside in the late spring caused his heart to well up with emotion and inspired this hymn.

Each stanza thanks God for a different kind of beauty. In its original form it was a Communion hymn of eight stanzas. Each stanza concluded with the words "Christ our God, to thee we raise this our sacrifice of praise," alluding to Hebrews 13:15.

Therefore,
LET US OFFER
through Jesus
A CONTINUAL SACRIFICE
of praise to God.
Hebrews 13:15

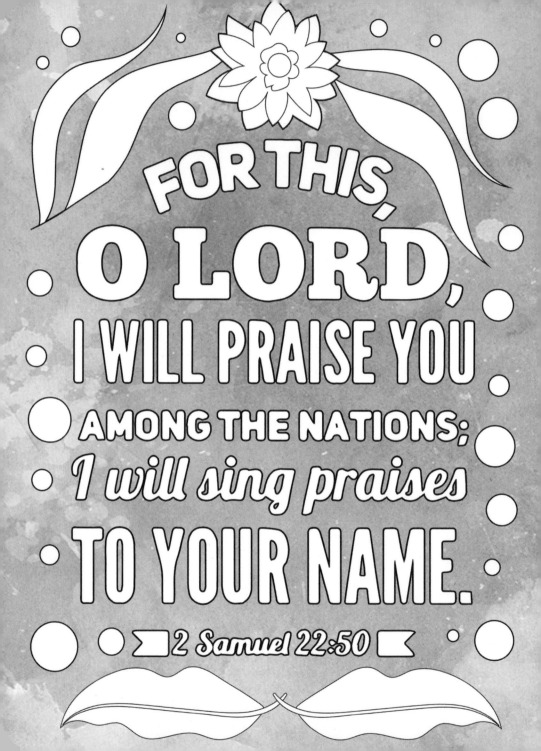

God of Our Fathers

They did not conquer the land with their swords; it was not their own strong arm that gave them victory. It was your right hand and strong arm and the blinding light from your face that helped them, for you loved them.

Psalm 44:3

God of our fathers, whose almighty hand
Leads forth in beauty all the starry band
Of shining worlds in splendor through the skies,
Our grateful songs before Thy throne arise.

Refresh Thy people on their toilsome way;
Lead us from night to never-ending day;
Fill all our lives with love and grace divine,
And glory, laud, and praise be ever Thine.

DANIEL CRANE ROBERTS (1841–1907)

SIX YEARS before his death in 1907, Daniel Roberts wrote, "I remain a country parson, known only within my own small world." This hymn was penned while he pastored a rural church in Brandon, Vermont. He wrote it in 1876 to commemorate the one-hundredth birthday of the Declaration of Independence, and it was sung for the first time at Brandon's Fourth of July celebration.

Because the people of Brandon enjoyed the hymn, Roberts submitted it to the committee planning the Constitution's centennial celebration. The committee chose it as the official hymn for the occasion and sent it to the organist at St. Thomas Episcopal Church in New York City to compose an original tune. The new tune, with a dramatic trumpet fanfare, helped to make this hymn unique.

It was your RIGHT HAND AND STRONG ARM AND THE BLINDING LIGHT from your face THAT HELPED THEM. PSALM 44:3

GRACE GREATER THAN OUR SIN

God's law was given so that all people could see how sinful they were. But as people sinned more and more, God's wonderful grace became more abundant. So just as sin ruled over all people and brought them to death, now God's wonderful grace rules instead, giving us right standing with God and resulting in eternal life through Jesus Christ our Lord.

Romans 5:20-21

Marvelous grace of our loving Lord,
Grace that exceeds our sin and our guilt!
Yonder on Calvary's mount outpoured—
There where the blood of the Lamb was spilt.

Grace, grace, God's grace,
Grace that will pardon and cleanse within,
Grace, grace, God's grace,
Grace that is greater than all our sin!

Marvelous, infinite, matchless grace,
Freely bestowed on all who believe!
You that are longing to see His face,
Will you this moment His grace receive?

JULIA HARRIETTE JOHNSTON (1849–1919)

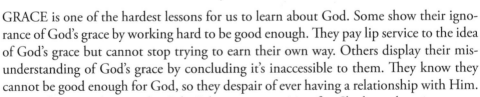

GRACE is one of the hardest lessons for us to learn about God. Some show their ignorance of God's grace by working hard to be good enough. They pay lip service to the idea of God's grace but cannot stop trying to earn their own way. Others display their misunderstanding of God's grace by concluding it's inaccessible to them. They know they cannot be good enough for God, so they despair of ever having a relationship with Him.

It is this second group that Julia Johnston was writing for. She knew how important it was to understand and experience the simple, yet difficult, truth of God's gracious forgiveness. Though she penned texts for more than five hundred hymns, this is the only one widely known.

But as people sinned
more and more,
God's wonderful
grace became
more abundant.
Romans 5:20

GUIDE ME, O THOU GREAT JEHOVAH

The LORD will guide you continually, giving you water when you are dry and restoring your strength. You will be like a well-watered garden, like an ever-flowing spring.

Isaiah 58:11

Guide me, O Thou great Jehovah,
Pilgrim through this barren land;
I am weak, but Thou art mighty;
Hold me with Thy powerful hand;
Bread of heaven, Bread of heaven,
Feed me till I want no more,
Feed me till I want no more.

Open now the crystal fountain,
Whence the healing stream doth flow;
Let the fire and cloudy pillar
Lead me all my journey through;
Strong deliverer, strong deliverer,
Be Thou still my strength and shield,
Be Thou still my strength and shield.

When I tread the verge of Jordan,
Bid my anxious fears subside;
Death of death and hell's destruction,
Land me safe on Canaan's side;
Songs of praises, songs of praises
I will ever give to Thee,
I will ever give to Thee.

WILLIAM WILLIAMS (1717–1791)
STANZA 1 TRANSLATED FROM THE WELSH
BY PETER WILLIAMS (1722–1796)
STANZAS 2 AND 3 PROBABLY TRANSLATED
BY THE AUTHOR

WOULDN'T YOU LIKE to know what next December holds in store for you? But it's still January! God leads us a day at a time, a step at a time. No need to worry about distant events. The Welsh hymn writer William Williams compared the Christian life to the Israelites' trek through the wilderness. We may not know the route by which God is leading us, but we humbly count on His guidance.

58

Hallelujah, What a Savior!

There was nothing beautiful or majestic about his appearance, nothing to attract us to him. He was despised and rejected—a man of sorrows, acquainted with deepest grief. We turned our backs on him and looked the other way.

Isaiah 53:2-3

"Man of Sorrows!" what a name
For the Son of God, who came
Ruined sinners to reclaim!
Hallelujah, what a Savior!

Guilty, vile and helpless we,
Spotless Lamb of God was He;
Full atonement! can it be?
Hallelujah, what a Savior!

Lifted up was He to die,
"It is finished!" was His cry;
Now in heav'n exalted high:
Hallelujah, what a Savior!

When He comes, our glorious King,
All His ransomed home to bring,
Then anew this song we'll sing:
Hallelujah, what a Savior!

Philip Paul Bliss (1838–1876)

PHILIP BLISS was one of the most prominent hymn writers in the heyday of gospel hymn writing. Bliss grew up working on a farm and in lumber camps, but eventually became a music teacher. He sold his first song at age twenty-six and later worked for a hymn publisher. D. L. Moody urged Bliss to become a singing evangelist, and so he did, beginning in 1874. This hymn was published in 1875. In 1876, while traveling through Ohio, Bliss and his family were involved in a train wreck. Reportedly, Bliss went back into the fiery train to save his wife, but they both died.

It was a tragedy for hymn lovers around the world, but you might say that Bliss just changed his address. Certainly he continues, even now, creating new praises for our wonderful Savior in glory.

Now in heav'n
EXALTED HIGH:
HALLELUJAH,
what a Savior!

Have Thine Own Way, Lord!

I . . . found the potter working at his wheel. But the jar he was making did not turn out as he had hoped, so he crushed it into a lump of clay again and started over. Then the Lord gave me this message: "O Israel, can I not do to you as this potter has done to his clay? As the clay is in the potter's hand, so are you in my hand."

Jeremiah 18:3-6

Have Thine own way, Lord! Have Thine own way!
Thou art the potter; I am the clay.
Mold me and make me after Thy will,
While I am waiting, yielded and still.

Have Thine own way, Lord! Have Thine own way!
Hold o'er my being absolute sway!
Fill with Thy Spirit till all shall see
Christ only, always, living in me!

ADELAIDE ADDISON POLLARD (1862–1934)

AT FORTY, Adelaide Pollard was trying unsuccessfully to raise support to go to Africa as a missionary. She wondered why the Lord could so burden her with the needs of Africa but not make it possible for her to go. During this time of discouragement, she attended a small prayer meeting where an elderly woman prayed, "Lord, it doesn't matter what You bring into our lives, just have Your way with us."

That night Pollard went home and read the story of Jeremiah's visit to the potter's house, and later that evening she wrote this hymn. She said that she had always felt the Lord was molding her and preparing her for His service. Then all of a sudden, He seemed to have deserted her.

"Perhaps," she reasoned, "my questioning of God's will shows a flaw in my life. So God decided to break me, as the potter broke the defective vessel, and then to mold my life again in His own pattern."

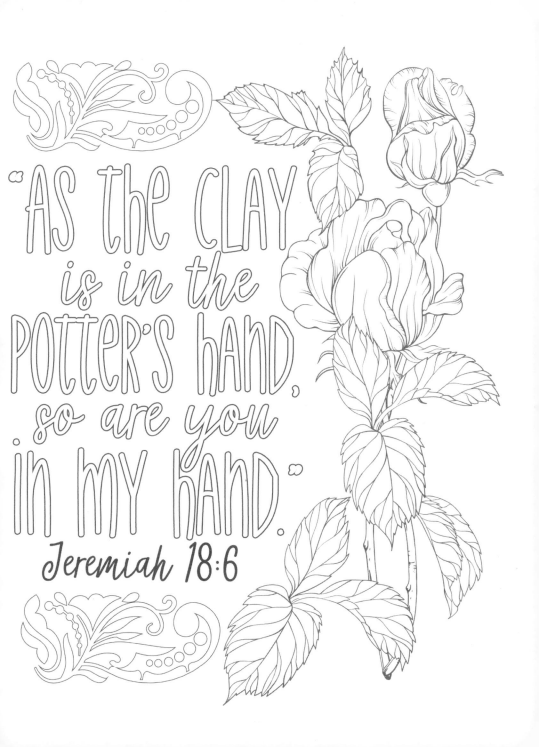

"As the CLAY
is in the
POTTER'S hand,
so are you
in my hand."

Jeremiah 18:6

He Giveth More Grace

Dear brothers and sisters, when troubles . . . come your way, consider it an opportunity for great joy. For you know that when your faith is tested, your endurance has a chance to grow.

James 1:2-3

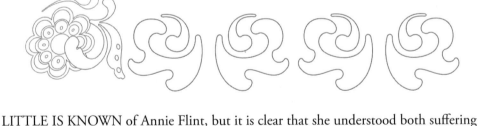

He giveth more grace when the burden grows greater;
He sendeth more strength when the labors increase.
To added affliction He addeth His mercy;
To multiplied trials, His multiplied peace.

His love has no limit;
His grace has no measure;
His pow'r has no boundary known unto men.
For out of His infinite riches in Jesus,
He giveth, and giveth, and giveth again!

When we have exhausted our store of endurance,
When our strength has failed ere the day is half done,
When we reach the end of our hoarded resources,
Our Father's full giving is only begun.

ANNIE JOHNSON FLINT (1866–1932)

LITTLE IS KNOWN of Annie Flint, but it is clear that she understood both suffering and grace. The apostle Paul understood these things, too. During his life of ministry in service of Christ, Paul was persecuted, imprisoned, beaten, and even stoned. And as if that weren't enough, he also suffered from an unidentified "thorn in the flesh"—a weakness that he could not overcome.

But amidst all his trials, Paul wrote, "Three different times I begged the Lord to take [the thorn] away. Each time he said, 'My grace is all you need. My power works best in weakness.' So now I am glad to boast about my weaknesses, so that the power of Christ can work through me" (2 Corinthians 12:8-9). Paul discovered that God's grace and power were sufficient to overcome any trial or weakness he might encounter.

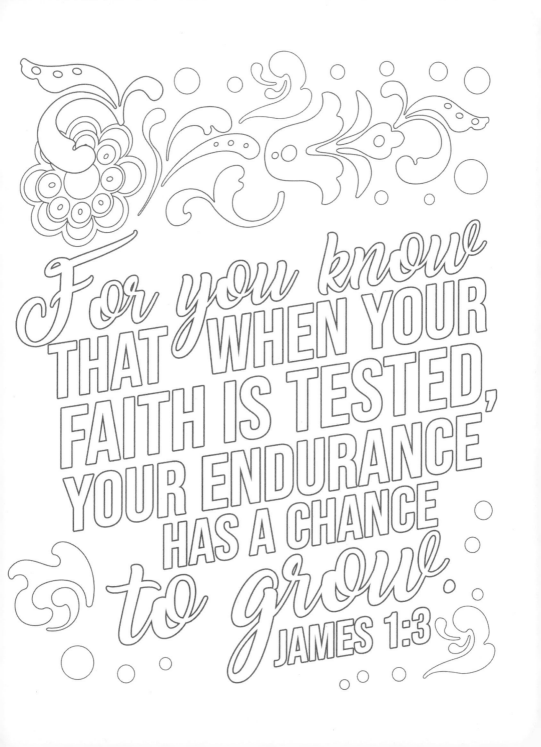

He Leadeth Me!

He leadeth me! O blessed thought!
O words with heav'nly comfort fraught!
Whate'er I do, where'er I be,
Still 'tis God's hand that leadeth me!

He leadeth me, He leadeth me,
By His own hand He leadeth me:
His faithful follower I would be,
For by His hand He leadeth me.

Lord, I would clasp Thy hand in mine,
Nor ever murmur nor repine,
Content, whatever lot I see,
Since 'tis Thy hand that leadeth me!

And when my task on earth is done,
When, by Thy grace, the vict'ry's won,
E'en death's cold wave I will not flee,
Since God through Jordan leadeth me!

JOSEPH HENRY GILMORE (1834–1918)

THE CIVIL WAR was being waged, and the outcome was still uncertain. Joseph Gilmore, pastor of Philadelphia's First Baptist Church, wanted to turn his people's attention to the security of God's guidance. The important thing, he said, is to know that God is leading—no matter *how* or *where* He leads us. After the service, Gilmore went to a deacon's home, and the conversation continued to revolve around the blessedness of God's leading. As others went on talking, he took out a pencil and wrote the words of this hymn, gave it to his wife, and forgot about it.

Three years later he was a pastoral candidate for a church in Rochester, New York. Since he was unfamiliar with the church's hymnal, he began leafing through it and spotted the hymn "He Leadeth Me"—his own hymn! Without his knowledge, Mrs. Gilmore had sent the words to a Christian periodical, which had them set to music.

For the honor
OF YOUR NAME,
lead me out
OF THIS DANGER.
Psalm 31:3

Holy, Holy, Holy

Holy, holy, holy! Lord God Almighty!
Early in the morning our song shall rise to Thee;
Holy, holy, holy! merciful and mighty!
God in three Persons, blessed Trinity!

Holy, holy, holy! all the saints adore Thee,
Casting down their golden crowns around the glassy sea;
Cherubim and seraphim falling down before Thee,
Which wert and art and evermore shalt be.

Holy, holy, holy! Lord God Almighty!
All Thy works shall praise Thy name in earth and sky and sea;
Holy, holy, holy! merciful and mighty!
God in three Persons, blessed Trinity!

REGINALD HEBER (1783–1826)

REGINALD HEBER was always trying to improve the music at the Anglican church he served in Hodnet, England. Though his superiors frowned on the use of anything but metrical psalms, Heber introduced hymns by Newton and Cowper and even wrote new hymns of his own. This one would impress Alfred, Lord Tennyson as the world's greatest hymn.

After serving sixteen years as a parish priest in England, Heber accepted the call to become the bishop of Calcutta, India. Whether in England, as he surveyed the prevalence of vice, or in India, where he was surrounded by the worship of false gods, Heber was impressed with the holiness of God. "Only Thou art holy," he wrote. The tune to which this hymn is usually sung is called "Nicaea," named after the church council that met in AD 325, which formulated the Nicene Creed and affirmed the doctrine of the Trinity.

"Holy, holy, holy is the Lord God, the Almighty."

Revelation 4:8

AND EACH MORNING
AND EVENING
THEY STOOD BEFORE
THE LORD
TO SING SONGS
OF THANKS
AND PRAISE TO HIM.
1 CHRONICLES 23:30

How Sweet the Name of Jesus Sounds

Jesus is the one referred to in the Scriptures, where it says, "The stone that you builders rejected has now become the cornerstone." There is salvation in no one else! God has given no other name under heaven by which we must be saved.

Acts 4:11-12

How sweet the name of Jesus sounds
In a believer's ear!
It soothes his sorrows, heals his wounds,
And drives away his fear.

It makes the wounded spirit whole
And calms the troubled breast;
'Tis manna to the hungry soul
And to the weary, rest.

Till then I would Thy love proclaim
With ev'ry fleeting breath;
And may the music of Thy name
Refresh my soul in death.

JOHN NEWTON (1725–1807)

AT THE AGE of eighty, John Newton was quite deaf and almost blind, but he still continued to preach. For his final messages, Newton brought an aide to the pulpit. The aide would read the next point of Newton's sermon outline, and Newton would then expound on that point.

On one particular Sunday, not long before Newton's death, the assistant read the first point and Newton said to the congregation, "Jesus Christ is precious." He paused and waited until the aide read the second point. Newton said again, "Jesus Christ is precious."

The aide reminded Newton that he had already said that. "Yes, I said it twice," the aged pastor replied, "and I'll say it again! Jesus Christ is precious." Then he asked the congregation to sing the hymn he had written many years before, "How Sweet the Name of Jesus Sounds."

GOD HAS GIVEN NO OTHER NAME UNDER HEAVEN BY WHICH WE MUST BE SAVED.

ACTS 4:12

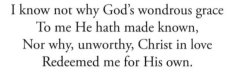

I Know Whom I Have Believed

I know not why God's wondrous grace
To me He hath made known,
Nor why, unworthy, Christ in love
Redeemed me for His own.

But "I know whom I have believed,
And am persuaded that He is able
To keep that which I've committed
Unto Him against that day."

I know not how this saving faith
To me He did impart,
Nor how believing in His Word
Wrought peace within my heart.

I know not when my Lord may come,
At night or noonday fair,
Nor if I'll walk the vale with Him,
Or "meet Him in the air."

DANIEL WEBSTER WHITTLE (1840–1901)

AS A POW during the Civil War, Daniel Whittle began reading the New Testament his mother had given him as he marched off to war, and he committed his life to Jesus Christ.

After the war, Whittle was promoted to the rank of major and then became a successful businessman. In 1873 he began preaching in evangelistic services, and for a quarter-century he led revivals throughout the United States. He also encouraged some of the leading songwriters of his time and wrote many hymns himself, including "Showers of Blessing" and "Moment by Moment." Whittle penned this hymn in 1883, perhaps thinking back to questions he had asked during his imprisonment. There were still many things he didn't know, but he certainly did know Jesus.

I Love Thy Kingdom, Lord

God has given me the responsibility of serving his church by proclaiming his entire message to you. This message was kept secret for centuries and generations past, but now it has been revealed to God's people.

Colossians 1:25-26

I love Thy kingdom, Lord,
The house of Thine abode,
The Church our blest Redeemer saved
With His own precious blood.

I love Thy Church, O God!
Her walls before Thee stand
Dear as the apple of Thine eye,
And graven on Thy hand.

For her my tears shall fall,
For her my prayers ascend,
To her my cares and toils be given,
Till toils and cares shall end.

Sure as Thy truth shall last,
To Zion shall be given
The brightest glories earth can yield,
And brighter bliss of heaven.

TIMOTHY DWIGHT (1752–1817)

LIKE HIS GRANDFATHER theologian Jonathan Edwards, Timothy Dwight was a brilliant scholar. He could read Latin when he was six, graduated from Yale at seventeen, began teaching there at nineteen, and wrote his first book at twenty.

He enlisted in the Continental Army in 1777 as a chaplain, where he became known for writing songs to encourage the troops. After the Revolutionary War, he served as a pastor in Connecticut. Finally, in 1795, he accepted the trustees' invitation to become president of Yale.

When Dwight returned to Yale, there were probably as few as five professing Christians on campus. But with Dwight came a new spiritual emphasis, and revival soon swept over the university. This hymn, written during the revivals at Yale, is the earliest American hymn in use today.

God has given me
THE RESPONSIBILITY
of serving
HIS CHURCH
BY PROCLAIMING
his entire message
TO YOU
COLOSSIANS 1:25

Immortal, Invisible, God Only Wise

Immortal, invisible, God only wise,
In light inaccessible hid from our eyes,
Most blessed, most glorious, the Ancient of Days,
Almighty, victorious, Thy great name we praise.

Unresting, unhasting, and silent as light,
Nor wanting, nor wasting, Thou rulest in might.
Thy justice like mountains high soaring above
Thy clouds which are fountains of goodness and love.

Great Father of glory, pure Father of light,
Thine angels adore Thee, all veiling their sight.
All praise we would render: O help us to see
'Tis only the splendor of light hideth Thee.

WALTER CHALMERS SMITH (1824–1908)

THE GREAT BRITISH hymnologist Erik Routley calls this hymn "full of plump polysyllables." The hymn was inspired by the apostle Paul's words to young Timothy: "Now unto the King eternal, immortal, invisible, the only wise God, be honour and glory for ever and ever" (1 Timothy 1:17, KJV). The writer of this hymn, Walter Chalmers Smith, was a pastor in the Free Church of Scotland for forty-four years (1850–1894). Smith wrote many hymns, but this is the only one still in use today.

I Need Thee Every Hour

Bend down, O Lord, and hear my prayer; answer me, for I need your help. Protect me, for I am devoted to you. Save me, for I serve you and trust you. You are my God. Be merciful to me, O Lord, for I am calling on you constantly. Give me happiness, O Lord, for I give myself to you.

Psalm 86:1-4

I need Thee ev'ry hour,
Most gracious Lord;
No tender voice like Thine
Can peace afford.

I need Thee, O I need Thee;
Ev'ry hour I need Thee!
O bless me now, my Savior,
I come to Thee.

I need Thee ev'ry hour,
In joy or pain;
Come quickly, and abide,
Or life is vain.

ANNIE SHERWOOD HAWKS (1835–1918)
ROBERT LOWRY (1826–1899), REFRAIN

YOU DON'T OFTEN THINK of hymns being written by thirty-seven-year-old homemakers from Brooklyn, but that's the story of this hymn. Annie Hawks was busy with her household chores when the words came to her. She later wrote, "I was so filled with a sense of nearness to my Master that, wondering how one could live without Him in either joy or pain, these words, 'I need thee every hour,' were flashed into my mind. Seating myself by the open window in the balmy air of the bright June day, I caught up my pencil and the words were soon committed to paper."

Hawks reflected, "It was not until years later, when the shadow fell over my way, the shadow of a great loss, that I understood something of the comforting power in the words." God often allows us to learn in the sunshine what we will need to lean on in the darkness.

I Sing the Mighty Power of God

I sing the mighty pow'r of God,
That made the mountains rise;
That spread the flowing seas abroad,
And built the lofty skies.
I sing the wisdom that ordained
The sun to rule the day;
The moon shines full at His command,
And all the stars obey.

There's not a plant or flow'r below,
But makes Thy glories known:
And clouds arise, and tempests blow,
By order from Thy throne;
While all that borrows life from Thee
Is ever in Thy care.
And ev'rywhere that man can be,
Thou, God, art present there.

ISAAC WATTS (1674–1748)

ISAAC WATTS never married, yet he loved children. In his own childhood, he was precocious. He learned Latin when he was four, Greek when he was eight or nine, French when he was eleven, and Hebrew when he was thirteen. As an adult, he not only wrote books on theology, but on psychology, logic, and astronomy as well. He also wrote a book of children's songs, which included this hymn, even though it was considered a hymn for adults. His *Divine and Moral Songs for Children* was the first hymnal written for children and remained popular for more than a hundred years.

I Surrender All

I once thought these things were valuable, but now I consider them worthless because of what Christ has done. Yes, everything else is worthless when compared with the infinite value of knowing Christ Jesus my Lord. For his sake I have discarded everything else, counting it all as garbage, so that I could gain Christ.

Philippians 3:7-8

All to Jesus I surrender,
All to Him I freely give;
I will ever love and trust Him,
In His presence daily live.

I surrender all,
I surrender all.
All to Thee, my blessed Savior,
I surrender all.

All to Jesus I surrender,
Lord, I give myself to Thee;
Fill me with Thy love and power,
Let Thy blessing fall on me.

JUDSON W. VAN DEVENTER (1855–1939)

MANY CHRISTIANS have sung this song with their fingers crossed. But J. W. Van DeVenter meant it. He was a schoolteacher by profession but an artist at heart. Teaching school allowed him to make a living while he continued his study of drawing and painting. After evangelistic meetings in his church, friends saw his gifts in counseling and working with people and urged him to become an evangelist. For five years he wavered between his love of art and what seemed to be God's calling to evangelistic ministry.

He later recalled, "At last the pivotal hour of my life came and I surrendered all. A new day was ushered into my life. I became an evangelist and discovered down deep in my soul a talent hitherto unknown to me." A few years later, Van DeVenter, remembering that decisive moment, wrote this hymn.

For his sake
I have discarded
everything else,
counting it all as garbage,
so that I could
GAIN CHRIST.
Philippians 3:8

It Is Well with My Soul

When peace like a river attendeth my way,
When sorrows like sea-billows roll;
Whatever my lot, Thou hast taught me to say,
"It is well, it is well with my soul."

*It is well with my soul,
It is well, it is well with my soul.*

And, Lord, haste the day when the faith shall be sight,
The clouds be rolled back as a scroll,
The trump shall resound and the Lord shall descend,
"Even so"—it is well with my soul.

HORATIO GATES SPAFFORD (1828–1888)

KNOWING that his friend Dwight L. Moody was going to be preaching in evangelistic campaigns in England in the fall of 1871, Horatio G. Spafford decided to take his family to England. His wife and four daughters went ahead on the SS *Ville du Havre,* and he planned to follow in a few days.

But on the Atlantic Ocean the ship was struck by an iron sailing vessel and sank within twelve minutes. Two hundred and twenty-six lives were lost—including the Spaffords' four daughters. When the survivors were brought to shore at Cardiff, Wales, Mrs. Spafford cabled her husband, "Saved alone."

Spafford booked passage on the next ship. As they were crossing the Atlantic, the captain pointed out the place where he thought the *Ville du Havre* had gone down. That night, Spafford penned the words "When sorrows like sea billows roll . . . it is well, it is well with my soul."

We can rejoice, too, when we run INTO PROBLEMS AND TRIALS, for we know that they HELP US DEVELOP ENDURANCE.

Romans 5:3

I WILL SING OF MY REDEEMER

Praise God for the glorious grace he has poured out on us who belong to his dear Son. He is so rich in kindness and grace that he purchased our freedom with the blood of his Son and forgave our sins.

Ephesians 1:6-7

I will sing of my Redeemer
And His wondrous love to me;
On the cruel cross He suffered,
From the curse to set me free.

Sing, O sing of my Redeemer,
With His blood He purchased me;
On the cross He sealed my pardon,
Paid the debt and made me free.

I will tell the wondrous story,
How, my lost estate to save,
In His boundless love and mercy,
He the ransom freely gave.

I will sing of my Redeemer
And His heav'nly love to me;
He from death to life hath bro't me,
Son of God with Him to be.

PHILIP PAUL BLISS (1838–1876)

IT'S NOT EASY to keep the Christian faith bottled up. Throughout history, various rulers have tried to keep Christians from preaching the gospel, but with little success. Ancient Rome would not have minded if Christians had just kept to themselves, privately enjoying their faith. But it doesn't work that way. As the apostles told the authorities in Jerusalem, "We cannot help speaking about what we have seen and heard" (Acts 4:20).

Bliss was the songleader for an evangelist known as Major Whittle, based in Chicago. This hymn text was found in Bliss's trunk after he and his wife died in a train accident in 1876. James McGranahan, who succeeded Bliss as Whittle's songleader, wrote the music and used it in their meetings.

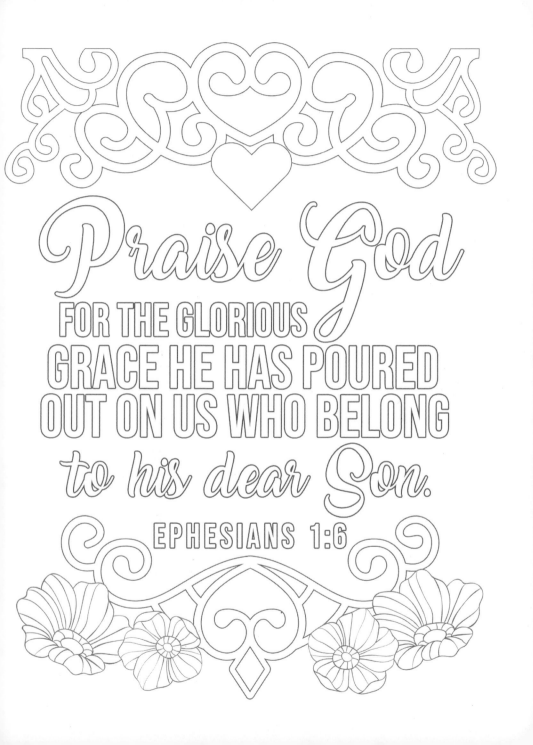

Praise God FOR THE GLORIOUS GRACE HE HAS POURED OUT ON US WHO BELONG to his dear Son.

EPHESIANS 1:6

Jesus, I Am Resting, Resting

So there is a special rest still waiting for the people of God. For all who have entered into God's rest have rested from their labors, just as God did after creating the world.

Hebrews 4:9-10

Jesus, I am resting, resting
In the joy of what Thou art;
I am finding out the greatness
Of Thy loving heart.
Thou hast bid me gaze upon Thee,
And Thy beauty fills my soul,
For by Thy transforming power,
Thou hast made me whole.

Jesus, I am resting, resting
In the joy of what Thou art;
I am finding out the goodness
Of Thy loving heart.

Ever lift Thy face upon me
As I work and wait for Thee;
Resting 'neath Thy smile, Lord Jesus,
Earth's dark shadows flee.
Brightness of my Father's glory,
Sunshine of my Father's face,
Keep me ever trusting, resting,
Fill me with Thy grace.

JEAN SOPHIA PIGOTT (1845–1882)

WE FIND IT DIFFICULT to be at rest—to be still—in a society that is always on the move. We live in a world of ten-second sound bites and short attention spans. We are taught to be dissatisfied with what we have and to strive for more.

In one of Christ's grandest invitations, He offered rest to the weary: "Come to me, all of you who are weary and carry heavy burdens, and I will give you rest" (Matthew 11:28). "In returning to me and resting in me will you be saved. In quietness and confidence is your strength," God told the Israelites in Isaiah 30:15.

If we focus on God, as this nineteenth-century British author did, we can rest, finding that He will satisfy our heart and its deepest longings, meet and supply our every need, and compass us around with blessings.

So there is a special REST STILL WAITING FOR THE PEOPLE of God.

Hebrews 4:9

Jesus, Lover of My Soul

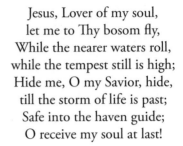

I am praying to you because
I know you will answer,
O God. Bend down and
listen as I pray. Show me
your unfailing love in wonderful ways. By your mighty
power you rescue those
who seek refuge from their
enemies. Guard me as you
would guard your own eyes.
Hide me in the shadow of
your wings.

Psalm 17:6-8

Jesus, Lover of my soul,
let me to Thy bosom fly,
While the nearer waters roll,
while the tempest still is high;
Hide me, O my Savior, hide,
till the storm of life is past;
Safe into the haven guide;
O receive my soul at last!

Other refuge have I none;
hangs my helpless soul on Thee;
Leave, ah! leave me not alone,
still support and comfort me.
All my trust on Thee is stayed;
all my help from Thee I bring;
Cover my defenseless head
with the shadow of Thy wing.

CHARLES WESLEY (1707–1788)

WRITTEN ONLY A YEAR after his conversion, this is one of the most famous of Charles Wesley's six thousand hymns. As he wrote it, he may have been remembering his turbulent transatlantic crossing three years earlier. He wrote in his journal, "The sea streamed in at the sides. . . . I rose and lay down by turns, but could remain in no posture long; strove vehemently to pray, but in vain." Later in the afternoon as the storm reached its peak, he said, "In this dreadful moment, I bless God, I found the comfort of hope."

Wesley talked to another passenger about trusting God, and the passenger replied that he had no refuge in times of danger. Even though Wesley was ill and frightened, he had the awareness, as he later wrote, that he "abode under the shadow of the Almighty."

Jesus Loves Me

Jesus loves me! this I know,
For the Bible tells me so;
Little ones to Him belong,
They are weak but He is strong.

Yes, Jesus loves me!
Yes, Jesus loves me!
Yes, Jesus loves me!
The Bible tells me so.

Jesus loves me! He who died
Heaven's gate to open wide;
He will wash away my sin,
Let His little child come in.

Jesus loves me! He will stay
Close beside me all the way;
Thou hast bled and died for me,
I will henceforth live for Thee.

ANNA BARTLETT WARNER (1820–1915)

ANNA WARNER and her sister, Susan, grew up near West Point Military Academy, where they became known for leading Sunday school services for the young men there. After the death of their father, a New York lawyer, the sisters supported themselves with their various literary endeavors. Susan became known as a bestselling novelist. Anna also wrote novels and published two collections of poems. She wrote this simple hymn in 1860 to be included in one of her sister's novels. In the story, it was a poem of comfort spoken to a dying child.

God sent
HIS SON
into the world
NOT TO JUDGE
the world,
BUT TO SAVE
the world
THROUGH HIM.
John 3:17

Jesus Paid It All

I hear the Savior say,
"Thy strength indeed is small!
Child of weakness, watch and pray,
Find in Me thine all in all."

Jesus paid it all,
All to Him I owe;
Sin had left a crimson stain—
He washed it white as snow.

Lord, now indeed I find
Thy pow'r, and Thine alone,
Can change the leper's spots
And melt the heart of stone.

And when before the throne
I stand in Him complete,
"Jesus died my soul to save,"
My lips shall still repeat.

ELVINA MABEL HALL (1820–1889)

WHAT DO YOU DO when the pastor rambles on too long? Elvina Hall wrote a hymn. Seated in the choir loft at the Monument Street Methodist Church of Baltimore, she had no paper to write on—only the flyleaf of the hymnal. There she wrote these stanzas.

The composer of the well-known tune to this hymn, John T. Grape, was the organist and choir director at the church. Professionally, he was a successful coal merchant, but he "dabbled in music," as he liked to say. He had come up with this tune, which he called "All to Christ I Owe."

It was the pastor, George Schrick, who put the words and tune together. Hall's stanzas fit part of Grape's tune, and she probably added the chorus to fit with his tune title.

Jesus Shall Reign

May the king's rule be refreshing like spring rain on freshly cut grass, like the showers that water the earth. May all the godly flourish during his reign. May there be abundant prosperity until the moon is no more. May he reign from sea to sea, and from the Euphrates River to the ends of the earth.

Psalm 72:6-8

Jesus shall reign where'er the sun
Does his successive journeys run;
His kingdom spread from shore to shore.
Till moons shall wax and wane no more.

Let every creature rise and bring
His grateful honors to our King;
Angels descend with songs again,
And earth repeat the loud amen!

ISAAC WATTS (1674–1748)

ISAAC WATTS once said that his aim was to see "David converted into a Christian." He meant singing the psalms was good but it would be better if they were infused with the gospel. He felt some psalms were unsuitable for Christian worship because they were written before the Cross of Christ and the completion of God's redemption and revelation.

The great missionary hymn "Jesus Shall Reign" is based on Psalm 72. There was no great mission effort when Watts wrote these words. Not until sixty years later did William Carey—the father of the modern missionary movement—sail for India. Today, by means of radio and literature, as well as through the work of faithful missionaries, Christ's kingdom has "spread from shore to shore."

Jesus, the Very Thought of Thee

Jesus, the very thought of Thee
With sweetness fills my breast;
But sweeter far Thy face to see,
And in Thy presence rest.

Nor voice can sing, nor heart can frame,
Nor can the mem'ry find
A sweeter sound than Thy blest name,
O Savior of mankind!

Jesus, our only joy be Thou,
As Thou our prize wilt be:
Jesus, be Thou our glory now,
And through eternity.

ATTRIBUTED TO BERNARD OF CLAIRVAUX (1091–1153)
TRANSLATED BY EDWARD CASWALL (1814–1878)

KNOWING GOD is a matter of the heart. This truth dominated the life of Bernard of Clairvaux. At a very early age Bernard was drawn to spiritual things, largely influenced by the piety of his mother. At twenty-two he entered a monastery at Citeaux, and three years later he founded a monastery at Clairvaux, serving as its spiritual leader until he died in 1153.

God's love was Bernard's lifeblood, pulsing through everything he said and did. His knowledge of God was deeply personal, a mystical love affair that not only gave meaning to his life on earth but formed his vision of heaven.

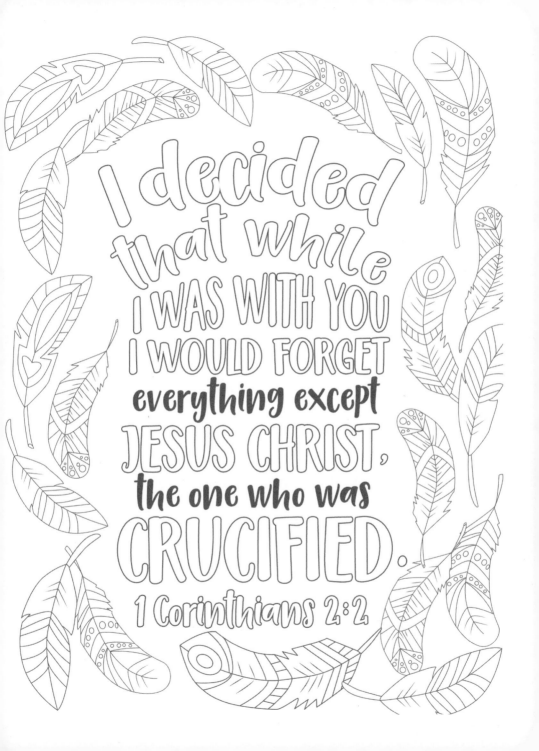

I decided that while I was with you I would forget everything except JESUS CHRIST, the one who was CRUCIFIED.

1 Corinthians 2:2

JESUS, THOU JOY OF LOVING HEARTS

On the last day, the climax of the festival, Jesus stood and shouted to the crowds, "Anyone who is thirsty may come to me! Anyone who believes in me may come and drink! For the Scriptures declare, 'Rivers of living water will flow from his heart.'"

John 7:37-38

Jesus, Thou joy of loving hearts!
Thou fount of life! Thou light of men!
From the best bliss that earth imparts,
We turn unfilled to Thee again.

Our restless spirits yearn for Thee
Where'er our changeful lot is cast,
Glad, when Thy gracious smile we see,
Blest, when our faith can hold Thee fast.

O Jesus, ever with us stay;
Make all our moments calm and bright;
Chase the dark night of sin away;
Shed o'er the world Thy holy light!

ATTRIBUTED TO BERNARD OF CLAIRVAUX (1091–1153)
TRANSLATED BY RAY PALMER (1808–1887)

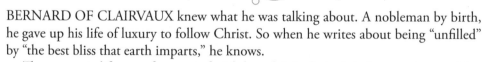

BERNARD OF CLAIRVAUX knew what he was talking about. A nobleman by birth, he gave up his life of luxury to follow Christ. So when he writes about being "unfilled" by "the best bliss that earth imparts," he knows.

The monastic life was often one of withdrawal. Monks had their own communities, which were largely self-sufficient. Thus they could work and pray in relative solitude. But Bernard broke out of that system and became an unusually public figure for a monk. He challenged popes and political leaders to live righteously. He urged professors to teach truth. He launched evangelistic campaigns.

We can learn much from Bernard's example. We do need time for "calm and bright" moments alone with Christ. But we also need to let Him send us forth in service.

JESUS, THY BLOOD AND RIGHTEOUSNESS

You know that God paid a ransom to save you from the empty life you inherited from your ancestors. And it was not paid with mere gold or silver . . . It was the precious blood of Christ, the sinless, spotless Lamb of God.

1 Peter 1:18-19

Jesus, Thy blood and righteousness
My beauty are, my glorious dress;
Midst flaming worlds, in these arrayed,
With joy shall I lift up my head.

Bold shall I stand in Thy great day,
For who aught to my charge shall lay?
Fully absolved through these I am,
From sin and fear, from guilt and shame.

Lord, I believe Thy precious blood,
Which, at the mercy seat of God,
Forever doth for sinners plead,
For me, e'en for my soul, was shed.

Lord, I believe were sinners more
Than sands upon the ocean shore,
Thou hast for all a ransom paid,
For all a full atonement made.

NICOLAUS VON ZINZENDORF (1700–1760)
TRANSLATED BY JOHN WESLEY (1703–1791)

COUNT NICOLAUS VON ZINZENDORF was one of the most remarkable persons in church history. He was born into a wealthy family in Saxony, Germany, educated at the best universities, and named counselor of the State of Saxony, but he chose to be associated with the Moravians, devout believers who had been exiled from Austria.

Of the two thousand hymns he wrote, this is perhaps the best known. His hymns were personal because he was a passionate promoter of what he called "Christianity of the heart." They were also Christ centered because his life motto was, "I have but one passion, and that is He and only He."

It was the precious BLOOD OF CHRIST, the sinless, SPOTLESS LAMB OF GOD.

1 Peter 1:19

JESUS! WHAT A FRIEND FOR SINNERS!

All praise to God, the Father of our Lord Jesus Christ, who has blessed us with every spiritual blessing in the heavenly realms because we are united with Christ. Even before he made the world, God loved us and chose us in Christ to be holy and without fault in his eyes. God decided in advance to adopt us into his own family by bringing us to himself through Jesus Christ.

Ephesians 1:3-5

Jesus! what a Friend for sinners!
Jesus! Lover of my soul;
Friends may fail me, foes assail me,
He, my Savior, makes me whole.

Jesus! I do now receive Him,
More than all in Him I find,
He hath granted me forgiveness,
I am His, and He is mine.

J. WILBUR CHAPMAN (1859–1918)

JESUS' DETRACTORS accused Him of being a friend of tax collectors and sinners. They couldn't have been more right.

In defense of His actions, Jesus said cryptically, "Wisdom is shown to be right by its results" (Matthew 11:19). Certainly He backed this up with His own actions. As He said later, "There is no greater love than to lay down one's life for one's friends" (John 15:13). That is precisely what He did for His friends, the sinners. Jesus gave His life so everyone can experience freedom from sin's powerful grip.

As a pastor and evangelist, J. Wilbur Chapman knew the joy of seeing scores of sinners open their hearts to the Lord. As a believer himself, he knew firsthand the joy of a sinner finding a friend in Christ.

GOD DECIDED IN ADVANCE TO ADOPT US INTO HIS OWN FAMILY BY BRINGING US TO HIMSELF through Jesus Christ.

EPHESIANS 1:5

Joyful, Joyful, We Adore Thee

*The heavens proclaim
the glory of God.
The skies display his
craftsmanship. Day after
day they continue to
speak; night after night
they make him known.
They speak without a
sound or word; their
voice is never heard.
Yet their message has
gone throughout the
earth, and their words
to all the world. God
has made a home in the
heavens for the sun.*

Psalm 19:1-4

Joyful, joyful, we adore Thee,
God of glory, Lord of love;
Hearts unfold like flowers before Thee,
Opening to the sun above.
Melt the clouds of sin and sadness;
Drive the dark of doubt away;
Giver of immortal gladness,
Fill us with the light of day!

All Thy works with joy surround Thee,
Earth and heav'n reflect Thy rays,
Stars and angels sing around Thee,
Center of unbroken praise;
Field and forest, vale and mountain,
Flowery meadow, flashing sea,
Chanting bird and flowing fountain,
Call us to rejoice in Thee.

Mortals join the mighty chorus,
Which the morning stars began;
Father love is reigning o'er us,
Brother love binds man to man.
Ever singing, march we onward,
Victors in the midst of strife;
Joyful music leads us sunward
In the triumph song of life.

HENRY VAN DYKE (1852–1933)

HENRY VAN DYKE was serving as a guest preacher at Williams College in the Berkshire Mountains of Massachusetts. He was so moved by the beauty of God's creation that he wrote this hymn of joy. The next morning he handed the poem to the college president. "Here is a hymn for you," he said. "Your mountains were my inspiration. It must be sung to the music of Beethoven's 'Hymn to Joy.'" And so it has been ever since.

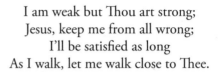

Just a Closer Walk with Thee

For God called you to do good, even if it means suffering, just as Christ suffered for you. He is your example, and you must follow in his steps.

1 Peter 2:21

I am weak but Thou art strong;
Jesus, keep me from all wrong;
I'll be satisfied as long
As I walk, let me walk close to Thee.

Just a closer walk with Thee,
Grant it, Jesus, is my plea,
Daily, walking close to Thee,
Let it be, dear Lord, let it be.

Through this world of toil and snares,
If I falter, Lord, who cares?
Who with me my burden shares?
None but Thee, dear Lord, none but Thee.

When my feeble life is o'er,
Time for me will be no more;
Guide me gently, safely o'er
To Thy kingdom shore, to Thy shore.

AUTHOR UNKNOWN

A FATHER left his son a note that read, "Will be in Far East on your birthday, but back Saturday with gift. What would you like—video game, bike, stereo?" The boy circled the item he wanted—"Saturday."

The boy could have chosen any plaything he wanted, but most of all he wanted to know his father. That's the heart of this familiar spiritual. "Just a closer walk with Thee," that's all we ask. As Paul said, "Everything else is worthless when compared with the infinite value of knowing Christ Jesus my Lord" (Philippians 3:8).

Fortunately, we don't have an "absentee" heavenly Father. He is there for us and will grant this request. He is happy to walk with us, to share our burdens, to guide us safely to the shore of His kingdom.

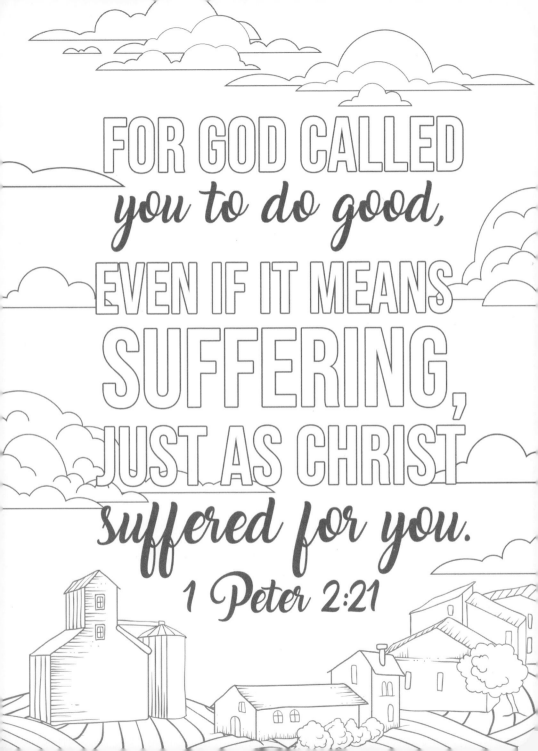

Just as I Am

Jesus replied, "I am the bread of life. Whoever comes to me will never be hungry again. Whoever believes in me will never be thirsty. . . . Those the Father has given me will come to me, and I will never reject them."

John 6:35, 37

Just as I am, without one plea,
But that Thy blood was shed for me,
And that Thou bidd'st me come to Thee,
O Lamb of God I come! I come!

Just as I am, and waiting not
To rid my soul of one dark blot,
To Thee, whose blood can cleanse each spot,
O Lamb of God I come! I come!

Just as I am, tho' tossed about
With many a conflict, many a doubt,
Fightings within, and fears without,
O Lamb of God I come! I come!

CHARLOTTE ELLIOTT (1789–1871)

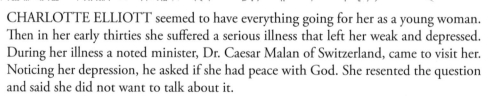

CHARLOTTE ELLIOTT seemed to have everything going for her as a young woman. Then in her early thirties she suffered a serious illness that left her weak and depressed. During her illness a noted minister, Dr. Caesar Malan of Switzerland, came to visit her. Noticing her depression, he asked if she had peace with God. She resented the question and said she did not want to talk about it.

But a few days later she went to apologize to Dr. Malan. She said that she wanted to clean up some things in her life before becoming a Christian. Malan looked at her and answered, "Come just as you are." That was enough for Charlotte Elliott, and she yielded herself to the Lord that day.

Fourteen years later, remembering those words spoken to her by Caesar Malan in Brighton, England, she wrote this simple hymn.

JESUS REPLIED, "I AM THE BREAD OF LIFE."

JOHN 6:35

Let Us Break Bread Together

Jesus said again, "I tell you the truth, unless you eat the flesh of the Son of Man and drink his blood, you cannot have eternal life within you. But anyone who eats my flesh and drinks my blood has eternal life, and I will raise that person at the last day."

John 6:53-54

Let us break bread together on our knees;
Let us break bread together on our knees;
When I fall on my knees
With my face to the rising sun,
O Lord, have mercy on me.

Let us drink the cup together on our knees;
Let us drink the cup together on our knees;
When I fall on my knees
With my face to the rising sun,
O Lord, have mercy on me.

Let us praise God together on our knees;
Let us praise God together on our knees;
When I fall on my knees
With my face to the rising sun,
O Lord, have mercy on me.

TRADITIONAL SPIRITUAL

SOME SAY THAT this spiritual was the password used to call slaves to secret, forbidden worship meetings in Virginia. Whether secret or not, the song calls Christians to gather and celebrate the Lord's Supper.

The posture is significant. Some churches have participants kneel to take the elements of Communion; others have them sit or stand. Whatever posture the body takes, the attitude of the heart is worship. We come in reverence before our Lord.

"The rising sun" could refer to an ancient custom of worshiping toward the east. Most cathedrals are built with the nave facing east. The rising sun has often been a symbol for God. It brings new life and light, a source of energy and hope.

"Anyone who eats my flesh and drinks my blood has eternal life, and I will raise that person at the last day." JOHN 6:54

Like a River Glorious

Oh, that you had listened to my commands! Then you would have had peace flowing like a gentle river and righteousness rolling over you like waves in the sea.

Isaiah 48:18

Like a river glorious
Is God's perfect peace,
Over all victorious
In its bright increase;
Perfect, yet it floweth
Fuller ev'ry day,
Perfect, yet it groweth
Deeper all the way.

Stayed upon Jehovah,
Hearts are fully blest—
Finding as He promised
Perfect peace and rest.

Ev'ry joy or trial
Falleth from above,
Traced upon our dial
By the sun of love;
We may trust Him fully
All for us to do—
They who trust Him wholly
Find Him wholly true.

FRANCES RIDLEY HAVERGAL
(1836–1879)

FRANCES RIDLEY HAVERGAL, a devout Bible scholar as well as a poet, drew upon two passages from the prophet Isaiah to give fresh understanding to Christian peace in difficult circumstances. More than once in Isaiah, God promises "peace like a river." And in Isaiah 26:3 the prophet says, "You will keep in perfect peace all who trust in you, all whose thoughts are fixed on you!" These verses have served as the basis of many hymns over the last two centuries, but none is as picturesque as this one.

THEN YOU WOULD HAVE

had peace

FLOWING

LIKE A GENTLE

river.

ISAIAH 48:18

Lord, Speak to Me

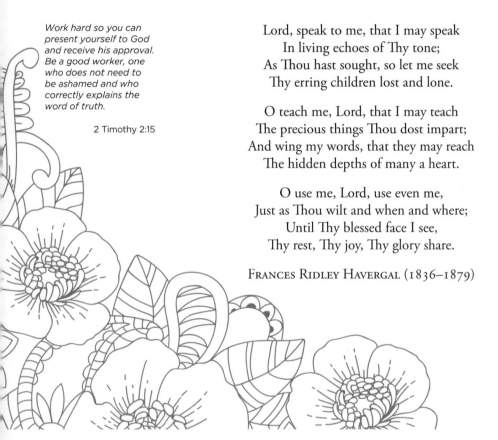

Lord, speak to me, that I may speak
In living echoes of Thy tone;
As Thou hast sought, so let me seek
Thy erring children lost and lone.

O teach me, Lord, that I may teach
The precious things Thou dost impart;
And wing my words, that they may reach
The hidden depths of many a heart.

O use me, Lord, use even me,
Just as Thou wilt and when and where;
Until Thy blessed face I see,
Thy rest, Thy joy, Thy glory share.

FRANCES RIDLEY HAVERGAL (1836–1879)

WHEN FRANCES HAVERGAL was a child, her father nicknamed her "Little Quicksilver." She had a quick and hungry mind and as a child memorized long passages of Scripture. Her mother died when Frances was only eleven, but one of the last things her mother said to her was, "Pray God to prepare you for all He is preparing for you."

Shortly before she wrote this hymn at the age of thirty-six, she wrote in a letter, "I am always getting surprised at my own stupidity. . . . If I am to write to any good, a great deal of living must go to a very little writing." About the same time, she also wrote, "I feel like a child writing. You know a child will look up at every sentence and ask, 'What shall I say next?' This is what I do. Every line and word and rhyme comes from God." She called this hymn "A Worker's Prayer."

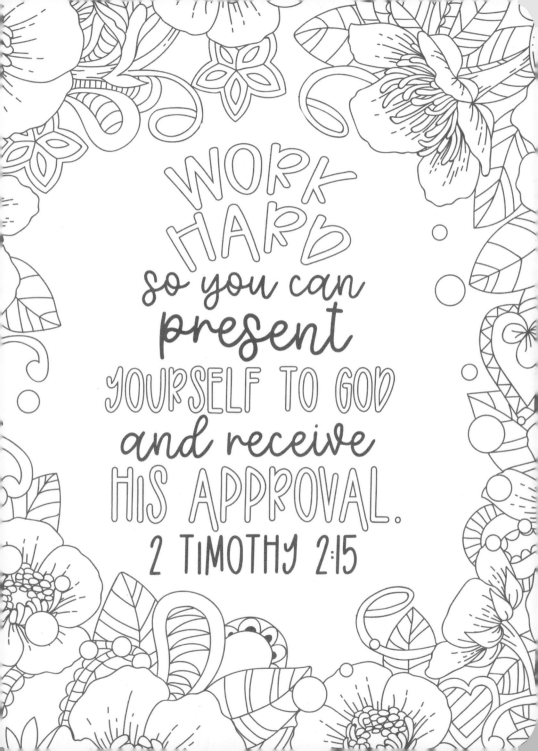

WORK HARD so you can present YOURSELF TO GOD and receive HIS APPROVAL.
2 TIMOTHY 2:15

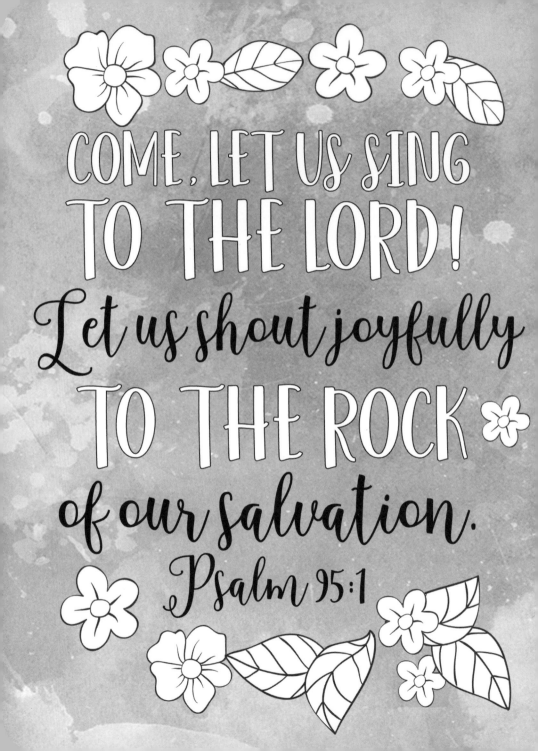

Love Divine, All Loves Excelling

We are eagerly waiting for [the Lord Jesus Christ] to return as our Savior. He will take our weak mortal bodies and change them into glorious bodies like his own, using the same power with which he will bring everything under his control.

Philippians 3:20-21

Love divine, all loves excelling,
Joy of heaven, to earth come down;
Fix in us Thy humble dwelling;
All Thy faithful mercies crown!
Jesus, Thou art all compassion,
Pure, unbounded love Thou art;
Visit us with Thy salvation;
Enter every trembling heart.

Breathe, O breathe Thy loving spirit
Into every troubled breast!
Let us all in Thee inherit;
Let us find that second rest.
Take away our bent to sinning;
Alpha and Omega be;
End of faith, as its beginning,
Set our hearts at liberty.

Finish, then, Thy new creation;
Pure and spotless let us be.
Let us see Thy great salvation
Perfectly restored in Thee:
Changed from glory into glory,
Till in heaven we take our place,
Till we cast our crowns before Thee,
Lost in wonder, love, and praise.

CHARLES WESLEY (1707–1788)

FOR MOST OF HIS LIFE Charles Wesley was a traveling preacher—traveling on horseback. In his pocket he carried little cards on which he scribbled hymns in shorthand as he rode.

Although Charles Wesley had been a classical scholar at Oxford, few of his hymns reveal allusions to the classics. However, this one follows the meter of John Dryden's "King Arthur," referring to Camelot: "Fairest Isle, all Isles excelling, Seats of pleasure and of love."

May the Mind of Christ, My Savior

May the mind of Christ, my Savior,
Live in me from day to day,
By His love and pow'r controlling
All I do and say.

May the word of God dwell richly
In my heart from hour to hour,
So that all may see I triumph
Only through His pow'r.

May the love of Jesus fill me
As the waters fill the sea;
Him exalting, self abasing—
This is victory.

May I run the race before me,
Strong and brave to face the foe,
Looking only unto Jesus
As I onward go.

May His beauty rest upon me
As I seek the lost to win,
And may they forget the channel,
Seeing only Him.

KATE B. WILKINSON (1859–1928)

MANY CHRISTIANS have made the New Year's resolution to be more like Jesus—but where do you start? The apostle Paul told the Philippian believers, "You must have the same attitude that Christ Jesus had" (Philippians 2:5). But how do we develop the attitude of Christ? Kate Wilkinson directs us to Colossians 3:16 for the answer: "Let the message about Christ, in all its richness, fill your lives." In the third stanza Wilkinson returns to Philippians for this promise: "God's peace . . . will guard your hearts and minds as you live in Christ Jesus" (Philippians 4:7). And so the song builds.

My Faith Has Found a Resting Place

My faith has found a resting place—
Not in device or creed:
I trust the Ever-Living One—
His wounds for me shall plead.

I need no other argument,
I need no other plea;
It is enough that Jesus died,
And that He died for me.

Enough for me that Jesus saves—
This ends my fear and doubt;
A sinful soul I come to Him—
He'll never cast me out.

My great Physician heals the sick—
The lost He came to save;
For me His precious blood He shed—
For me His life He gave.

LIDIE H. EDMUNDS (NINETEENTH CENTURY)

THE PIONEERING radio preacher Donald Grey Barnhouse used to ask, "When you get to the pearly gates and God asks, 'Why should I let you into My heaven?' what will you say?" This song is an answer to that question.

God does not run heaven like a country club or a successful corporation. We cannot get in on *our own* qualifications. The door is barred to all who try to earn their entry. But it swings wide open for the simple saint who affirms in faith, "I need no other argument, I need no other plea; it is enough that Jesus died, and that He died for me."

My Faith Looks Up to Thee

My faith looks up to Thee,
Thou Lamb of Calvary,
Savior divine!
Now hear me while I pray,
Take all my guilt away,
O let me from this day
Be wholly Thine!

May Thy rich grace impart
Strength to my fainting heart,
My zeal inspire;
As Thou hast died for me,
O may my love to Thee
Pure, warm, and changeless be,
A living fire!

When ends life's passing dream,
When death's cold, threatening stream
Shall o'er me roll,
Blest Savior, then, in love,
Fear and distrust remove;
O lift me safe above,
A ransomed soul!

RAY PALMER (1808–1887)

AT TWENTY-TWO, Ray Palmer was having a tough year. He wanted to go into the ministry but was stuck teaching in New York City. He was lonely, depressed, and sick. Then he found a German poem about a sinner kneeling before the cross. He translated it and added stanzas.

Two years later, while visiting Boston, he ran across his friend Lowell Mason. Mason, a major figure in American music in the early 1800s, was preparing a new hymnal. He asked Palmer if he'd like to contribute anything. Palmer bashfully showed Mason these verses. "You may live many years and do many good things," Mason said, "but I think you will be best known to posterity as the author of 'My Faith Looks Up to Thee.'"

My Hope Is Built on Nothing Less

If we are living in the light, as God is in the light, then we have fellowship with each other, and the blood of Jesus, his Son, cleanses us from all sin. If we claim we have no sin, we are only fooling ourselves and not living in the truth. But if we confess our sins to him, he is faithful and just to forgive us our sins and to cleanse us from all wickedness.

1 John 1:7-9

My hope is built on nothing less
Than Jesus' blood and righteousness;
I dare not trust the sweetest frame,
But wholly lean on Jesus' name.

On Christ, the solid rock, I stand;
All other ground is sinking sand,
All other ground is sinking sand.

When darkness veils His lovely face,
I rest on His unchanging grace;
In every high and stormy gale,
My anchor holds within the vale.

When He shall come with trumpet sound,
O may I then in Him be found!
Dressed in His righteousness alone,
Faultless to stand before the throne!

EDWARD MOTE (1797–1874)

MANY of the British hymn writers were children of the clergy or came from middle- or upper-class backgrounds. But not Edward Mote. His parents kept a pub in London, and Mote says, "My Sundays were spent in the streets; so ignorant was I that I did not know that there was a God." He was apprenticed to a cabinetmaker who took him to church, where he heard the gospel message. Mote himself became a successful cabinetmaker in a London suburb and was active in his local church.

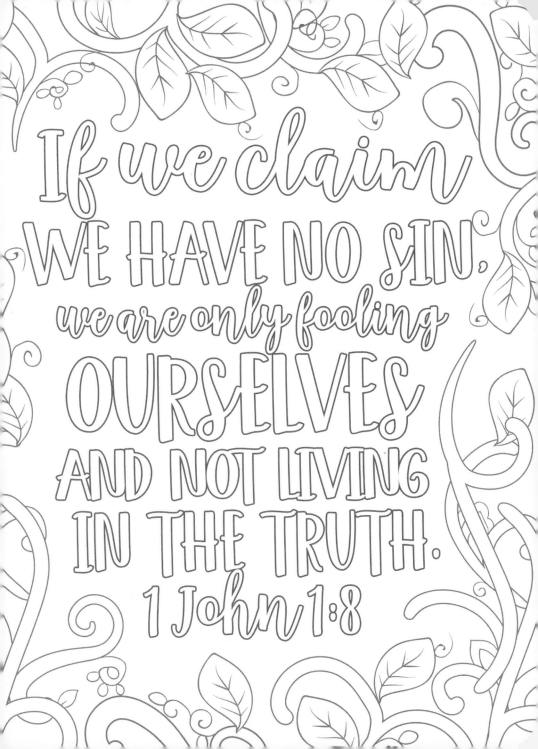

If we claim
WE HAVE NO SIN,
we are only fooling
OURSELVES
AND NOT LIVING
IN THE TRUTH.
1 John 1:8

My Jesus, I Love Thee

This is real love—not that we loved God, but that he loved us and sent his Son as a sacrifice to take away our sins. Dear friends, since God loved us that much, we surely ought to love each other.

1 John 4:10-11

My Jesus, I love Thee, I know Thou art mine—
For Thee all the follies of sin I resign;
My gracious Redeemer, my Savior art Thou:
If ever I loved Thee, my Jesus, 'tis now.

I love Thee because Thou hast first loved me
And purchased my pardon on Calvary's tree;
I love Thee for wearing the thorns on Thy brow:
If ever I loved Thee, my Jesus, 'tis now.

I'll love Thee in life, I will love Thee in death,
And praise Thee as long as Thou lendest me breath;
And say when the death-dew lies cold on my brow,
"If ever I loved Thee, my Jesus, 'tis now."

In mansions of glory and endless delight,
I'll ever adore Thee in heaven so bright;
I'll sing with the glittering crown on my brow,
"If ever I loved Thee, my Jesus, 'tis now."

WILLIAM RALPH FEATHERSTON (1846–1873)

SIXTEEN-YEAR-OLD William Featherston of Montreal wrote this simple hymn shortly after his conversion in 1862. He died before his twenty-seventh birthday, and this is apparently the only hymn he wrote.

Young Featherston sent the poem to his aunt in Los Angeles, who then sent it to England, where it appeared in *The London Hymnbook* of 1864. Back in Boston, Massachusetts, Baptist minister A. J. Gordon was preparing a hymnal for Baptist congregations when he saw "My Jesus, I Love Thee" in the British hymnal. He didn't like the music the words were set to, and he later wrote that "in a moment of inspiration, a beautiful new air sang itself to me." The simple tune he wrote perfectly complemented the simple words, and soon the hymn was being sung across America.

We surely OUGHT TO LOVE each other.

1 John 4:11

Nearer, My God, to Thee

Nearer, my God, to Thee, nearer to Thee!
E'en though it be a cross that raiseth me;
Still all my song shall be, nearer, my God, to Thee,
Nearer, my God, to Thee, nearer to Thee.

Or if on joyful wing, cleaving the sky,
Sun, moon, and stars forgot, upward I fly,
Still all my song shall be nearer, my God, to Thee,
Nearer, my God, to Thee, nearer to Thee.

SARAH FLOWER ADAMS (1805–1848)

SARAH ADAMS had to say farewell often, but she never liked it. Her mother had died when Sarah was only five—that was her first farewell. At thirty-two, as an actress playing Lady Macbeth in London's Richmond Theater, she said farewell to the stage. She wanted to continue, but her health was failing. The health of her sister was also poor, and Adams feared the day when she would have to bid her farewell. She began to question her faith. Why did God seem so far away?

When Adams's pastor asked her and her sister to help him prepare a hymnal, the two responded eagerly, writing thirteen texts and sixty-two new tunes. As the sisters were finishing their work, their pastor mentioned that he was planning a sermon about Jacob's dream of a ladder ascending to heaven and he needed an appropriate hymn. Adams soon completed "Nearer, My God, to Thee."

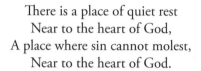

Near to the Heart of God

I know the LORD is always with me. I will not be shaken, for he is right beside me. No wonder my heart is glad, and I rejoice. My body rests in safety.

Psalm 16:8-9

There is a place of quiet rest
Near to the heart of God,
A place where sin cannot molest,
Near to the heart of God.

O Jesus, blest Redeemer,
Sent from the heart of God,
Hold us who wait before Thee
Near to the heart of God.

There is a place of comfort sweet
Near to the heart of God,
A place where we our Savior meet,
Near to the heart of God.

There is a place of full release
Near to the heart of God,
A place where all is joy and peace,
Near to the heart of God.

CLELAND BOYD MCAFEE (1866–1944)

WHERE DO YOU TURN when unexpected tragedy strikes? Cleland McAfee, a Presbyterian minister in Chicago, had just received word that his brother and sister-in-law had lost both of their daughters to diphtheria within twenty-four hours. Grief-stricken, McAfee couldn't think of deep theological issues; he could only think of verses in the book of Psalms that brought comfort and rest to those who sought refuge in the Lord. As he meditated on God's Word, he wrote the words and music to this simple hymn.

At the double funeral, outside the darkened, quarantined house of his brother, Cleland McAfee with a choking voice sang this hymn publicly for the first time. The following Sunday, his church choir sang it from their pastor's handwritten copy.

LET EVERYTHING
THAT BREATHES
sing
praises
TO THE LORD!
Praise the LORD!
PSALM 150:6

Now Thank We All Our God

Now thank we all our God
With heart and hands and voices,
Who wondrous things hath done,
In whom His world rejoices;
Who, from our mothers' arms,
Hath blessed us on our way
With countless gifts of love,
And still is ours today.

All praise and thanks to God
The Father now be given,
The Son, and Him who reigns
With them in highest heaven,
The one eternal God,
Whom earth and heaven adore;
For thus it was, is now,
And shall be evermore. Amen.

MARTIN RINKART (1586–1649)
TRANSLATED BY CATHERINE WINKWORTH (1827–1878)

WITH THE EXCEPTION of "A Mighty Fortress Is Our God," this is the most widely sung hymn in Germany. Like so many other great hymns, it was forged in the crucible of the Thirty Years' War. Martin Rinkart was the only pastor in the walled city of Eilenberg. In the crowded conditions, hunger and plague were chronic problems. In 1637 Rinkart conducted funerals for five thousand residents—including his wife.

Yet thanksgiving erupts from this stately song. The tune, by Johann Cruger, was introduced with the text in 1644 while the war still raged. It has a majesty and a resolve that few other works can match.

Thank the LORD!
Praise his name!

ISAIAH 12:4

Now the Day Is Over

Now the day is over,
Night is drawing nigh,
Shadows of the evening
Steal across the sky.

Jesus, give the weary
Calm and sweet repose;
With Thy tend'rest blessing
May our eyelids close.

Grant to little children
Visions bright of Thee;
Guard the sailors tossing
On the deep blue sea.

Thro' the long night-watches,
May Thine angels spread
Their white wings above me,
Watching round my bed.

When the morning wakens,
Then may I arise,
Pure and fresh and sinless
In Thy holy eyes.

SABINE BARING-GOULD (1834–1924)

SABINE BARING-GOULD wrote eighty-five books in areas as diverse as religion, travel, folklore, mythology, history, fiction, biography, sermons, and popular theology. He wrote a fifteen-volume *Lives of the Saints*. He edited a quarterly review of ecclesiastical art and literature. But he loved children, and we remember him best for his children's hymns: "Onward, Christian Soldiers" and "Now the Day Is Over."

YOU CAN GO TO BED WITHOUT FEAR; YOU WILL LIE DOWN AND SLEEP SOUNDLY.

PROVERBS 3 : 24

O for a Thousand Tongues to Sing

O for a thousand tongues to sing
my great Redeemer's praise,
The glories of my God and King,
the triumphs of His grace!

My gracious Master and my God,
assist me to proclaim,
To spread thro' all the earth abroad
the honors of Thy name.

He speaks, and listening to His voice,
new life the dead receive;
The mournful, broken hearts rejoice;
the humble poor believe.

Hear Him, ye deaf; His praise, ye dumb,
your loosened tongues employ;
Ye blind, behold your Savior come;
and leap, ye lame, for joy.

CHARLES WESLEY (1707–1788)

THE ORIGINAL TITLE of this hymn was "For the Anniversary Day of One's Conversion"; Charles Wesley wrote it on May 21, 1749, the eleventh anniversary of his own conversion. Before they were converted, John and Charles Wesley were dubbed "methodists" because of the methods of spirituality they had introduced in their club at Oxford, the Holy Club. But later John and Charles met the German Moravians, who loved to sing, were very missions-minded, and emphasized a personal conversion experience.

One of the Moravian leaders, Peter Bohler, once said, "Had I a thousand tongues, I would praise Christ Jesus with all of them." So it was fitting for Charles Wesley to build a hymn around that quotation to celebrate the date of his conversion.

When he comes, he will open the eyes of the blind and unplug the ears of the deaf.
Isaiah 35:5

O God, Our Help in Ages Past

Lord, through all the generations you have been our home! Before the mountains were born, before you gave birth to the earth and the world, from beginning to end, you are God. . . . For you, a thousand years are as a passing day, as brief as a few night hours.

Psalm 90:1-2, 4

O God, our help in ages past,
Our hope for years to come,
Our shelter from the stormy blast,
And our eternal home!

Time, like an ever-rolling stream,
Bears all its sons away;
They fly, forgotten, as a dream
Dies at the opening day.

O God, our help in ages past,
Our hope for years to come;
Be Thou our guide while life shall last,
And our eternal home.

ISAAC WATTS (1674–1748)

IN 1714, the people of England were anxious. Queen Anne lay dying, and she had no son or daughter to succeed her. Who would be the new monarch, and what changes would that make? Isaac Watts had reason to worry. His father had been imprisoned under the previous regime because his views did not please the ruling family. As a young child, Isaac had been carried by his mother to visit his father in jail. But Queen Anne had brought a new tolerance, and freedom for the elder Watts. Now that she was dying, what would happen?

Isaac Watts turned to Psalm 90 on this occasion and penned what may be the greatest of his more than six hundred hymns. The greatness of our eternal God was a favorite theme for Watts. When the events of the day bring worry, the God of the ages remains our eternal home.

150

O Love That Will Not Let Me Go

O Love that will not let me go,
I rest my weary soul in Thee;
I give Thee back the life I owe,
That in Thine ocean depths its flow
May richer, fuller be.

O Light that foll'west all my way,
I yield my flick'ring torch to Thee;
My heart restores its borrowed ray,
That in Thy sunshine's blaze its day
May brighter, fairer be.

GEORGE MATHESON (1842–1906)

GEORGE MATHESON went completely blind when he was eighteen years old. Still, he went on to become a great preacher in the Church of Scotland, assisted by his sister, who learned Greek and Hebrew to help with his research.

This hymn was written on the evening of June 6, 1882. Matheson later wrote, "It was the day of my sister's marriage. . . . Something happened to me, which was known only to myself, and which caused me the most severe mental suffering. The hymn was the fruit of that suffering."

What was it that happened to him? Some think he was remembering the time his fiancée broke their engagement when she learned that he was going blind. Or perhaps it was difficult for him to have his devoted sister getting married. In any case, he was led to ponder God's eternal love, which would turn his "flick'ring torch" into blazing daylight.

Open My Eyes, That I May See

Be good to your servant, that I may live and obey your word. Open my eyes to see the wonderful truths in your instructions. I am only a foreigner in the land. Don't hide your commands from me! I am always overwhelmed with a desire for your regulations.

Psalm 119:17-20

Open my eyes, that I may see
Glimpses of truth Thou hast for me;
Place in my hands the wonderful key,
That shall unclasp and set me free.
Silently now I wait for Thee,
Ready, my God, Thy will to see;
Open my eyes, illumine me,
Spirit divine!

Open my ears, that I may hear
Voices of truth Thou sendest clear;
And while the wave-notes fall on my ear,
Ev'rything false will disappear.
Silently now I wait for Thee,
Ready, my God, Thy will to see;
Open my ears, illumine me,
Spirit divine!

Open my mouth, and let it bear
Gladly the warm truth ev'rywhere;
Open my heart, and let me prepare
Love with Thy children thus to share.
Silently now I wait for Thee,
Ready, my God, Thy will to see;
Open my heart, illumine me,
Spirit divine!

CLARA H. SCOTT (1841–1897)

CLARA SCOTT was a music teacher who composed a great deal of instrumental and vocal music. She became known for her book of anthems, *The Royal Anthem Book,* which was published in 1882. Her productive life of composing and teaching at the Women's Seminary in Lyons, Iowa, is evidence that her eyes and ears were open to God's leading and that she was ready to share what God gave her. We should be ready to do the same.

O Sacred Head, Now Wounded

The soldiers took Jesus into the courtyard of the governor's headquarters (called the Praetorium) and called out the entire regiment. They dressed him in a purple robe, and they wove thorn branches into a crown and put it on his head. . . . And they struck him on the head with a reed stick, spit on him, and dropped to their knees in mock worship.

Mark 15:16-19

O sacred Head, now wounded,
With grief and shame weighed down,
Now scornfully surrounded
With thorns Thine only crown:
How pale Thou art with anguish,
With sore abuse and scorn!
How does that visage languish
Which once was bright as morn!

What language shall I borrow
To thank Thee, dearest Friend,
For this Thy dying sorrow,
Thy pity without end?
O make me Thine forever;
And should I fainting be,
Lord, let me never, never
Outlive my love to Thee.

ATTRIBUTED TO BERNARD OF CLAIRVAUX (1091–1153)
TRANSLATED FROM LATIN INTO GERMAN BY
PAUL GERHARDT (1607–1676)
TRANSLATED INTO ENGLISH BY
JOHN WADDELL ALEXANDER (1804–1859)

ALTHOUGH BERNARD was one of the most influential Christians of the Middle Ages, settling disputes between kings and influencing the selection of popes, he remained a devout monk, single-minded in his devotion to Christ.

"O Sacred Head, Now Wounded" comes from a poem originally having seven sections, each focusing on a wounded part of the crucified Savior's body—His feet, knees, hands, side, breast, heart, and head. The text of this hymn compels us to gaze at the cross until the depth of God's love overwhelms us. Bernard's hymn pictures God's love, not as an abstract theological statement, but as a profoundly personal and awesome vision of the suffering Christ.

LORD,
LET ME NEVER,
NEVER OUTLIVE
MY LOVE TO THEE.

O the Deep, Deep Love of Jesus

May you have the power to understand, as all God's people should, how wide, how long, how high, and how deep his love is. May you experience the love of Christ, though it is too great to understand fully.

Ephesians 3:18-19

O the deep, deep love of Jesus,
Vast, unmeasured, boundless, free!
Rolling as a mighty ocean
In its fullness over me,
Underneath me, all around me,
Is the current of Thy love;
Leading onward, leading homeward
To my glorious rest above.

O the deep, deep love of Jesus,
Spread His praise from shore to shore!
How He loveth, ever loveth,
Changeth never, nevermore;
How He watches o'er His loved ones,
Died to call them all His own;
How for them He intercedeth,
Watcheth o'er them from the throne.

O the deep, deep love of Jesus,
Love of every love the best;
'Tis an ocean vast of blessing,
'Tis a haven sweet of rest,
O the deep, deep love of Jesus,
'Tis a heav'n of heav'ns to me;
And it lifts me up to glory,
For it lifts me up to Thee.

SAMUEL TREVOR FRANCIS (1834–1925)

HOW DEEP is the love of Jesus? This hymn tries to express something of its magnitude. It is an ocean and more. It is a "heaven of heavens." But what does that mean? How does knowing of this deep, deep love affect the way we live each day?

Perhaps most important, it reassures us. When the apostle Paul says that nothing can separate us from the love of Christ, we know that even our own sin will not stop Jesus from loving us. He continually offers His loving forgiveness. Christ's love also motivates us.

O to Be Like Thee!

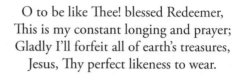

O to be like Thee! blessed Redeemer,
This is my constant longing and prayer;
Gladly I'll forfeit all of earth's treasures,
Jesus, Thy perfect likeness to wear.

O to be like Thee! O to be like Thee,
Blessed Redeemer, pure as Thou art!
Come in Thy sweetness, come in Thy fullness—
Stamp Thine own image deep on my heart.

O to be like Thee! while I am pleading,
Pour out Thy Spirit, fill with Thy love;
Make me a temple meet for Thy dwelling,
Fit me for life and heaven above.

THOMAS OBADIAH CHISHOLM (1866–1960)

WHEN PEOPLE WERE INTRODUCED to Thomas O. Chisholm, the author of this hymn and of "Great Is Thy Faithfulness," he would often say, "Aw, I'm just an old shoe!"

Chisholm was self-educated and began teaching in a rural school when he was sixteen. At the age of twenty-seven, the Kentucky farm boy wrote this hymn, "O to Be Like Thee!" He served on the staff of the *Pentecostal Herald* in Louisville until his health broke. He was accepted as a traveling preacher in the Methodist Church, but once again health problems caused him to resign. Regretfully he had to leave the ministry. Eventually he became a life insurance agent.

Throughout his life he displayed many of the characteristics that he praised in Jesus in the hymns he wrote. Chisholm, who described himself as an old shoe, was perhaps more like Christ than he realized.

WE DO KNOW THAT
WE WILL BE LIKE HIM,
FOR WE WILL SEE HIM
AS HE REALLY IS.
I JOHN 3:2

O Worship the King

Let all that I am praise
the LORD. O LORD my
God, how great you
are! You are robed with
honor and majesty. You
are dressed in a robe
of light. You stretch out
the starry curtain of the
heavens; you lay out the
rafters of your home
in the rain clouds. You
make the clouds your
chariot; you ride upon
the wings of the wind.
The winds are your mes-
sengers; flames of fire
are your servants.

Psalm 104:1-4

O worship the King, all glorious above,
O gratefully sing His power and His love;
Our Shield and Defender, the Ancient of Days,
Pavilioned in splendor, and girded with praise.

O tell of His might, O sing of His grace,
Whose robe is the light, whose canopy space;
His chariots of wrath the deep thunderclouds form,
And dark is His path on the wings of the storm.

Frail children of dust, and feeble as frail,
In Thee do we trust, nor find Thee to fail;
Thy mercies how tender, how firm to the end,
Our Maker, Defender, Redeemer, and Friend.

ROBERT GRANT (1779–1838)

SIR ROBERT GRANT was acquainted with kings. His father was a member of the British Parliament and later became chairman of the East India Company. Following in his father's footsteps, young Grant was elected to Parliament and then also became a director of the East India Company. In 1834 he was appointed governor of Bombay, and in that position he became greatly loved. A medical college in India was named in his honor.

This hymn by Grant is based on Psalm 104, a psalm of praise.

Praise, My Soul, the King of Heaven

Let all that I am praise
the LORD; with my whole
heart, I will praise his
holy name. Let all that
I am praise the LORD;
may I never forget the
good things he does for
me. He forgives all my
sins and heals all my
diseases.

Psalm 103:1-3

Praise, my soul, the King of heaven,
To His feet thy tribute bring;
Ransomed, healed, restored, forgiven,
Evermore His praises sing.
Alleluia! Alleluia! Praise the everlasting King.

Praise Him for His grace and favor
To our fathers in distress;
Praise Him, still the same as ever,
Slow to chide, and swift to bless,
Alleluia! Alleluia! Glorious in His faithfulness.

Fatherlike, He tends and spares us;
Well our feeble frame He knows;
In His hands He gently bears us,
Rescues us from all our foes.
Alleluia! Alleluia! Widely yet His mercy flows.

Angels in the height, adore Him;
Ye behold Him face to face;
Saints triumphant, bow before Him,
Gathered in from every race.
Alleluia! Alleluia! Praise with us the God of grace.

HENRY FRANCIS LYTE (1793–1847)

IN 1834 the British clergyman Henry Francis Lyte published a collection of 280 hymns based on the book of Psalms. He called it *The Spirit of the Psalms* because these hymns were not strictly translations (like the old psalters still in use at that time) or even paraphrases (like much of Isaac Watts's work), but texts loosely inspired by the psalms. This hymn was included as a development of Psalm 103. There are many points of comparison.

Queen Elizabeth II chose this hymn to be sung at her wedding in 1947. It is an apt song for any occasion, as we join our voices in this great "Alleluia!"

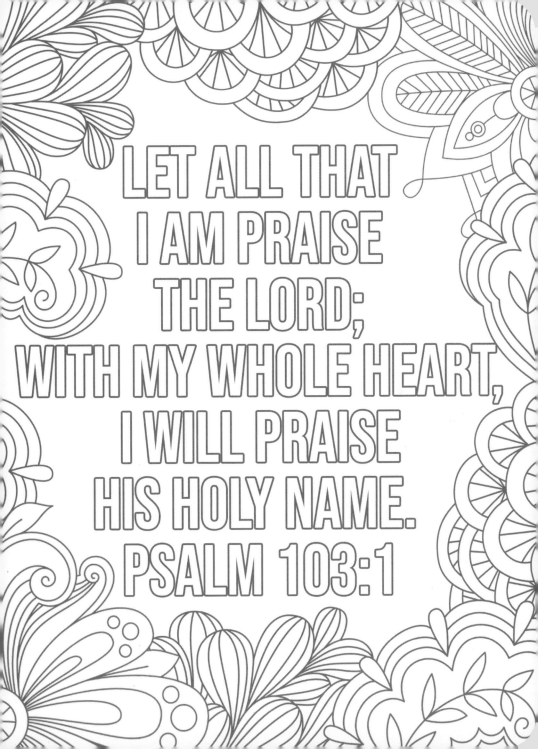

Praise the Savior, Ye Who Know Him

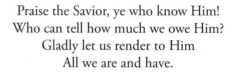

Because we are united with Christ, we have received an inheritance from God, for he chose us in advance, and he makes everything work out according to his plan.

Ephesians 1:11

Praise the Savior, ye who know Him!
Who can tell how much we owe Him?
Gladly let us render to Him
All we are and have.

Jesus is the name that charms us,
He for conflict fits and arms us;
Nothing moves and nothing harms us
While we trust in Him.

Keep us, Lord, O keep us cleaving
To Thyself, and still believing,
Till the hour of our receiving
Promised joys with Thee.

Then we shall be where we would be,
Then we shall be what we should be;
Things that are not now, nor could be,
Soon shall be our own.

THOMAS KELLY (1769–1855)

THERE WAS NOTHING wishy-washy about Thomas Kelly. He was an Irishman through and through, from Kellywatle, Ireland. He studied to be a lawyer like his father, but in the process began to read Christian doctrine. Under conviction of sin, he struggled to find peace with God through fasting and asceticism, but it didn't work. Eventually, he trusted Jesus Christ for the free gift of salvation through faith. He was ordained a minister in the established church, but because of his strong views on salvation by grace, he moved on to serve in independent chapels.

It is said that most of his hymns were focused on Jesus Christ, praising Him for His work on the cross and the glories of heaven. This hymn is typical of Kelly, beginning with grateful praise to his Savior and ending with a meditation on heaven.

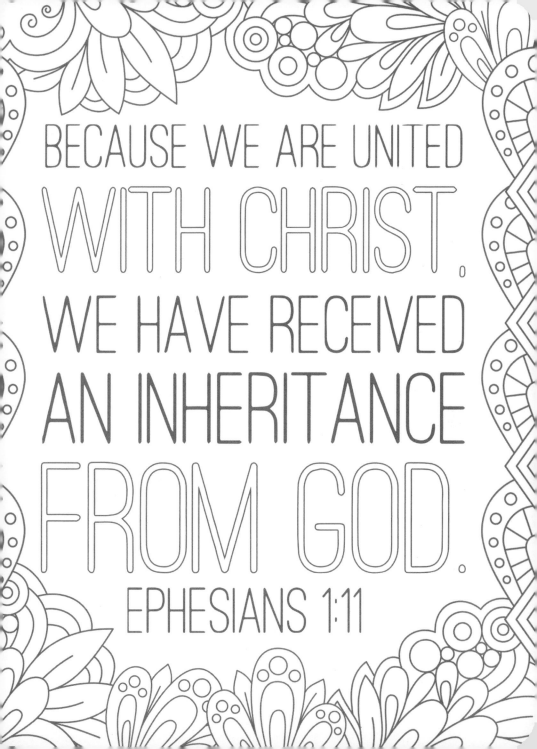

PRAISE TO THE LORD, THE ALMIGHTY

Praise to the Lord, the Almighty, the King of creation!
O my soul, praise Him, for He is thy health and salvation!
All ye who hear, now to His temple draw near;
Join me in glad adoration!

Praise to the Lord, who o'er all things so wondrously reigneth,
Shieldeth thee under His wings, yea, so gently sustaineth!
Hast thou not seen how thy desires e'er have been
Granted in what He ordaineth?

Praise to the Lord! O let all that is in me adore Him!
All that hath life and breath, come now with praises before Him!
Let the amen sound from His people again;
Gladly forever adore Him.

JOACHIM NEANDER (1650–1680)
TRANSLATED BY CATHERINE WINKWORTH (1827–1878)

AS A STUDENT in Bremen, Germany, Joachim Neander lived a godless life. Then, when Neander was twenty, a preacher named Under-Eyke came to Bremen and Neander was converted.

Four years later he became headmaster of a school in Düsseldorf, and during his time there he wrote more than sixty hymns. Because of his strong Christian views and his evangelistic activities, he displeased the authorities and was eventually removed from his position.

Despite the tensions, he wrote many hymns of praise. He often wandered through the valleys and hills near Düsseldorf, communing with his Lord. After losing his position at the school, he lived for a time in a cave and continued to write hymns. He died very young, at the age of thirty, but he left behind him a legacy of praise to God.

ROCK OF AGES

Rock of Ages, cleft for me,
Let me hide myself in Thee;
Let the water and the blood,
From Thy wounded side which flowed,
Be of sin the double cure,
Save from wrath and make me pure.

While I draw this fleeting breath,
When my eyes shall close in death,
When I rise to worlds unknown,
And behold Thee on Thy throne,
Rock of Ages, cleft for me,
Let me hide myself in Thee.

AUGUSTUS TOPLADY (1740–1778)

CONVERTED under a Methodist evangelist while attending the University of Dublin, Augustus Toplady decided to prepare for the ministry. Though impressed with the spirit of Methodism, he strongly disagreed with the Wesleys' Arminian theology and waged a running battle with them through tracts, sermons, and even hymns. "Wesley," said Toplady, "is guilty of Satan's shamelessness." Wesley retorted, "I do not fight with chimney sweeps!"

Toplady wrote "Rock of Ages" to conclude a magazine article in which he emphasized that, just as England could never repay its national debt, so humans through their own efforts could never satisfy the eternal justice of God. He died of tuberculosis and overwork at the age of thirty-eight, two years after he published his own hymnal, in which "Rock of Ages" and Charles Wesley's "Jesus, Lover of My Soul" were placed side by side.

Savior, Like a Shepherd Lead Us

Savior, like a shepherd lead us,
Much we need Thy tender care;
In Thy pleasant pastures feed us,
For our use Thy folds prepare:
Blessed Jesus, blessed Jesus!
Thou hast bought us, Thine we are.

We are Thine, do Thou befriend us,
Be the guardian of our way;
Keep Thy flock, from sin defend us,
Seek us when we go astray:
Blessed Jesus, blessed Jesus!
Hear, O hear us, when we pray.

Early let us seek Thy favor,
Early let us do Thy will;
Blessed Lord and only Savior,
With Thy love our bosoms fill:
Blessed Jesus, blessed Jesus!
Thou hast loved us, love us still.

HYMNS FOR THE YOUNG, 1836
ATTRIBUTED TO DOROTHY A. THRUPP (1779–1847)

OF ALL THE NAMES and titles given to Jesus, perhaps the most beloved is *Shepherd,* a title Jesus gave Himself in John 10. The Good Shepherd knows His sheep, guards His sheep, and even gives His life for His sheep. Scripture also says that He knows His sheep by name.

Unfortunately we don't know the author of this hymn by name. The hymn was first published in a book of songs and poems by Dorothy Thrupp of Paddington Green, England. The poems that she contributed are followed by her initials, D.A.T., but this one has no initials. Either she forgot to initial it, or it came from another source. Dorothy Thrupp's book was *Hymns for the Young,* and so the hymn is often identified as a children's hymn, though its message applies to people of all ages.

"I AM THE GOOD SHEPHERD; *I know my own sheep,* AND THEY KNOW ME."

JOHN 10:14

Softly and Tenderly Jesus Is Calling

Softly and tenderly Jesus is calling,
Calling for you and for me;
See, on the portals He's waiting and watching,
Watching for you and for me.

Come home, come home,
Ye who are weary, come home;
Earnestly, tenderly, Jesus is calling,
Calling, O sinner, come home!

Why should we tarry when Jesus is pleading,
Pleading for you and for me?
Why should we linger and heed not His mercies,
Mercies for you and for me?

Time is now fleeting, the moments are passing,
Passing from you and from me;
Shadows are gathering, death's night is coming,
Coming for you and for me.

O for the wonderful love He has promised,
Promised for you and for me!
Though we have sinned, He has mercy and pardon,
Pardon for you and for me.

WILLIAM LAMARTINE THOMPSON (1847–1909)

WILL THOMPSON was called the bard of Ohio. From his home in East Liverpool, Ohio, he went to New York City to sell some of the secular songs he had written. Music dealers picked them up, and soon people across the country were singing "My Home on the Old Ohio" and "Gathering Shells from the Seashore."

But Thompson, a Christian, soon began concentrating on hymn writing and set up his own firm for publishing hymnals. Sometime around 1880, when Thompson was thirty-three years old, he wrote this invitation hymn, "Softly and Tenderly."

Stand Up, Stand Up for Jesus

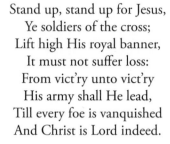

A final word: Be strong in the Lord and in his mighty power. Put on all of God's armor so that you will be able to stand firm against all strategies of the devil.

Ephesians 6:10-11

Stand up, stand up for Jesus,
Ye soldiers of the cross;
Lift high His royal banner,
It must not suffer loss:
From vict'ry unto vict'ry
His army shall He lead,
Till every foe is vanquished
And Christ is Lord indeed.

Stand up, stand up for Jesus,
The strife will not be long.
This day the noise of battle;
The next, the victor's song.
To him that overcometh,
A crown of life shall be;
He with the King of Glory
Shall reign eternally.

GEORGE DUFFIELD JR. (1818–1888)

IN 1858, churches throughout Philadelphia united in a citywide evangelistic effort. Every morning and evening, services were held in churches, convention halls, and theaters. Dudley Tyng, a twenty-nine-year-old Episcopalian preacher, spoke to five thousand men; one thousand responded to the gospel invitation.

Four days later, however, Tyng was fatally injured in an accident. As he lay dying, his fellow ministers gathered around him. Tyng was still thinking about the men who had made decisions for Christ and in his last, whispered words said, "Tell them to stand up for Jesus."

Presbyterian minister George Duffield preached the next Sunday on the text "Stand therefore" and in conclusion read a poem that he had just written entitled "Stand Up for Jesus." A church member sent the poem to a Baptist newspaper, where it was eventually published.

PUT ON ALL OF GOD'S ARMOR
SO THAT YOU WILL BE ABLE
TO STAND FIRM
AGAINST ALL STRATEGIES
OF THE DEVIL.
EPHESIANS 6:11

Sweet Hour of Prayer

Pray in the Spirit at
all times and on every
occasion. Stay alert and
be persistent in your
prayers for all believers
everywhere.

Ephesians 6:18

Sweet hour of prayer! sweet hour of prayer!
That calls me from a world of care,
And bids me at my Father's throne
Make all my wants and wishes known;
In seasons of distress and grief,
My soul has often found relief,
And oft escaped the tempter's snare,
By thy return, sweet hour of prayer!

Sweet hour of prayer! sweet hour of prayer!
Thy wings shall my petition bear
To Him whose truth and faithfulness
Engage the waiting soul to bless;
And since He bids me seek His face,
Believe His Word and trust His grace,
I'll cast on Him my every care,
And wait for thee, sweet hour of prayer!

WILLIAM W. WALFORD (1772–1850)

ACCORDING TO ONE ACCOUNT, the author of this hymn was a blind preacher and curio shop owner in Coleshill, England. He carved ornaments out of ivory or wood and sold them in his small store. He also wrote poetry. One day, when a local minister stopped at the store, William Walford, the blind shop owner, mentioned that he had composed a poem in his head. He asked the minister to write it down for him. Three years later, that minister visited the United States and gave the poem to a newspaper editor.

Unfortunately, no one knows what happened to William Walford of Coleshill. Researchers have found a William Walford, a minister of Homerton, England, who wrote a book on prayer that expresses many of the same thoughts that are given in this poem. That may be the true author. But the identity of the hymn writer is not as important as knowing a God who hears and answers prayer.

Take My Life and Let It Be

Take my life and let it be
Consecrated, Lord, to Thee;
Take my moments and my days—
Let them flow in ceaseless praise,
Let them flow in ceaseless praise.

Take my will and make it Thine—
It shall be no longer mine;
Take my heart—it is Thine own,
It shall be Thy royal throne,
It shall be Thy royal throne.

Take my love—my Lord, I pour
At Thy feet its treasure store;
Take myself—and I will be
Ever, only, all for Thee,
Ever, only, all for Thee.

FRANCES RIDLEY HAVERGAL (1836–1879)

THE PROLIFIC British hymn writer Frances Ridley Havergal wrote this hymn on February 4, 1874. "I went for a little visit of five days to Areley House," she explained. "There were ten persons in the house, some unconverted and long prayed for, some converted but not rejoicing Christians. He gave me the prayer, 'Lord, give me all in this house!' And He just did. Before I left the house, everyone had got a blessing. The last night of my visit I was too happy to sleep, and passed most of the night in praise and renewal of my own consecration, and these little couplets formed themselves and chimed in my heart one after another, till they finished with 'Ever, only, ALL for Thee.'" As Frances wrote the words she capitalized *ALL*.

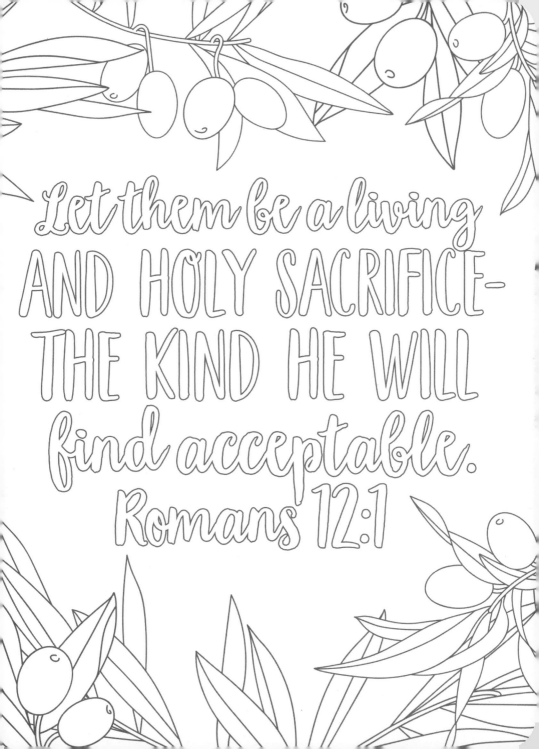

Thanks to God for My Redeemer

Thanks to God for my Redeemer,
Thanks for all Thou dost provide!
Thanks for times now but a memory,
Thanks for Jesus by my side!
Thanks for pleasant, balmy springtime,
Thanks for dark and dreary fall!
Thanks for tears by now forgotten,
Thanks for peace within my soul!

Thanks for roses by the wayside,
Thanks for thorns their stems contain!
Thanks for home and thanks for fireside,
Thanks for hope, that sweet refrain!
Thanks for joy and thanks for sorrow,
Thanks for heav'nly peace with Thee!
Thanks for hope in the tomorrow,
Thanks through all eternity!

AUGUST LUDWIG STORM (1862–1914)
TRANSLATED BY CARL E. BACKSTROM (1901–1984)

IT IS EASY to thank God for roses. It is much harder to thank Him for the thorns. This hymn offers a mature approach to thanksgiving, showing appreciation for pain and pleasure, joy and sorrow.

August Storm wrote this hymn in 1891 while still a young man of twenty-nine. He worked for the Salvation Army in Sweden and published this hymn in the organization's periodical, *The War Cry.*

Just eight years after writing this hymn, Storm was stricken with a back problem that left him crippled for the rest of his life. He managed to continue his Salvation Army work, and he maintained a thankful spirit even during this most difficult time. If anything, his troubles gave more power and credibility to his sermons and writings.

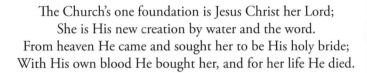

Together, we are his house, built on the foundation of the apostles and the prophets. And the cornerstone is Christ Jesus himself.

Ephesians 2:20

The Church's one foundation is Jesus Christ her Lord;
She is His new creation by water and the word.
From heaven He came and sought her to be His holy bride;
With His own blood He bought her, and for her life He died.

Elect from every nation, yet one o'er all the earth,
Her charter of salvation, one Lord, one faith, one birth;
One holy name she blesses, partakes one holy food,
And to one hope she presses, with every grace endued.

Yet she on earth hath union with God the Three in One,
And mystic sweet communion with those whose rest is won.
O happy ones and holy! Lord, give us grace that we,
Like them, the meek and lowly, on high may dwell with Thee.

SAMUEL JOHN STONE (1839–1900)

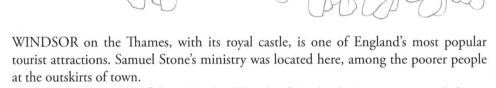

WINDSOR on the Thames, with its royal castle, is one of England's most popular tourist attractions. Samuel Stone's ministry was located here, among the poorer people at the outskirts of town.

Samuel Stone was a fighter. In the Church of England, Stone was regarded as a fundamentalist, opposing the liberal theological tendencies of his day. When he was twenty-seven, he wrote a collection of hymns based on the Apostles' Creed. This hymn, taken from that collection, is based on the article in the Creed regarding the church as the body of Christ.

Two years later, Anglicans from around the world met to discuss the crucial theological issues that were raging in the church. Significantly, they chose Stone's hymn as the processional for their historic conference.

The Lord's My Shepherd, I'll Not Want

The LORD is my shepherd; I have all that I need. He lets me rest in green meadows; he leads me beside peaceful streams. He renews my strength. He guides me along right paths, bringing honor to his name.

Psalm 23:1-3

The Lord's my Shepherd, I'll not want;
He makes me down to lie
In pastures green; He leadeth me
The quiet waters by.

My soul He doth restore again;
And me to walk doth make
Within the paths of righteousness,
E'en for His own name's sake.

Yea, though I walk through death's dark vale,
Yet will I fear no ill;
For Thou art with me, and Thy rod
And staff me comfort still.

My table Thou hast furnished
In presence of my foes;
My head Thou dost with oil anoint,
And my cup overflows.

Goodness and mercy all my life
Shall surely follow me;
And in God's house forevermore
My dwelling place shall be.

SCOTTISH PSALTER, 1650

SCOTTISH BIBLES in the seventeenth century often had psalms in meter printed after the book of Revelation. The metrical psalms were sung twice a day in most of the humble cottages of Scotland and so became more familiar to the people than the Bible text itself.

This text of the familiar Twenty-third Psalm comes from a metrical version by Francis Rous, a member of the British Parliament. He was dissatisfied with the accuracy of other psalm translations being used by the Puritans, some of which took liberties with the meaning to make the words rhyme. As you can see, this version is a faithful paraphrase of David's original.

The Old Rugged Cross

He did not retaliate when he was insulted, nor threaten revenge when he suffered. He left his case in the hands of God, who always judges fairly. He personally carried our sins in his body on the cross so that we can be dead to sin and live for what is right.

1 Peter 2:23-24

On a hill far away stood an old rugged cross,
The emblem of suffering and shame;
And I love that old cross where the dearest and best
For a world of lost sinners was slain.

So I'll cherish the old rugged cross,
'Til my trophies at last I lay down;
I will cling to the old rugged cross,
And exchange it some day for a crown.

O that old rugged cross, so despised by the world,
Has a wondrous attraction for me;
For the dear Lamb of God left His glory above
To bear it to dark Calvary.

To the old rugged cross I will ever be true,
Its shame and reproach gladly bear;
Then He'll call me some day to my home far away,
Where His glory forever I'll share.

George Bennard (1873–1958)

"THE INSPIRATION came to me one day in 1913, when I was staying in Albion, Michigan," George Bennard wrote about the composition of this hymn. "I began to write 'The Old Rugged Cross.' I completed the melody first. The words that I first wrote were imperfect. The words of the finished hymn were put into my heart in answer to my own need. Shortly thereafter it was introduced at special meetings in Pokagon, Michigan, on June 7, 1913."

After its debut at Pokagon, the song was presented at an evangelistic convention in Chicago. Participants then took it back to their homes throughout the country.

AND I LOVE THAT
OLD CROSS WHERE
THE DEAREST AND BEST
FOR A WORLD
OF LOST SINNERS
WAS SLAIN.

There Is a Fountain Filled with Blood

On that day a fountain will be opened for the dynasty of David and for the people of Jerusalem, a fountain to cleanse them from all their sins and impurity.

Zechariah 13:1

There is a fountain filled with blood
Drawn from Emmanuel's veins,
And sinners, plunged beneath that flood,
Lose all their guilty stains,
Lose all their guilty stains;
And sinners, plunged beneath that flood,
Lose all their guilty stains.

Then in a nobler, sweeter song,
I'll sing Thy pow'r to save,
When this poor lisping, stammering tongue
Lies silent in the grave,
Lies silent in the grave;
When this poor lisping, stammering tongue
Lies silent in the grave.

WILLIAM COWPER (1731–1800)

WILLIAM COWPER suffered from deep depression for most of his life. In 1764 he found himself within the walls of an institution for the mentally ill. There in the asylum, William Cowper found Christ through reading the Bible.

Despite his emotional pain, or perhaps because of it, Cowper produced literature of amazing insight. He is still renowned in literary circles as one of England's greatest poets.

ON THAT DAY A FOUNTAIN
WILL BE OPENED FOR THE DYNASTY
OF DAVID AND FOR THE PEOPLE
OF JERUSALEM,
A FOUNTAIN TO CLEANSE
THEM FROM ALL THEIR SINS
AND IMPURITY.
ZECHARIAH 13:1

Sing PSALMS and hymns and SPIRITUAL SONGS to GOD with thankful hearts.

Colossians 3:16

This Is My Father's World

This is my Father's world,
And to my listening ears
All nature sings, and round me rings
The music of the spheres.
This is my Father's world:
I rest me in the thought
Of rocks and trees, of skies and seas—
His hand the wonders wrought.

This is my Father's world,
The birds their carols raise,
The morning light, the lily white,
Declare their Maker's praise.
This is my Father's world:
He shines in all that's fair;
In the rustling grass I hear Him pass,
He speaks to me everywhere.

This is my Father's world,
O let me ne'er forget
That though the wrong seems oft so strong,
God is the Ruler yet.
This is my Father's world:
The battle is not done;
Jesus who died shall be satisfied,
And earth and heav'n be one.

Mᴀʟᴛʙɪᴇ Dᴀᴠᴇɴᴘᴏʀᴛ Bᴀʙᴄᴏᴄᴋ (1858–1901)

MALTBIE BABCOCK was an athlete. An outstanding baseball pitcher and a champion swimmer, he kept himself in shape by running. When he was pastor of the First Presbyterian Church in Lockport, New York, he would run out in the early morning to the brow of the hill two miles away and look over at Lake Ontario. Before he left, he would tell his church staff, "I am going out to see my Father's world." From the brow of the hill, he would run two more miles to a deep ravine where as many as forty different species of birds found a sanctuary. Then he would run back.

'Tis So Sweet to Trust in Jesus

'Tis so sweet to trust in Jesus,
Just to take Him at His Word,
Just to rest upon His promise,
Just to know "Thus saith the Lord."

Jesus, Jesus, how I trust Him!
How I've proved Him o'er and o'er!
Jesus, Jesus, precious Jesus!
O for grace to trust Him more!

O how sweet to trust in Jesus,
Just to trust His cleansing blood,
Just in simple faith to plunge me
'Neath the healing, cleansing flood!

Yes, 'tis sweet to trust in Jesus,
Just from sin and self to cease,
Just from Jesus simply taking
Life and rest and joy and peace.

I'm so glad I learned to trust Him,
Precious Jesus, Savior, Friend;
And I know that He is with me,
Will be with me to the end.

Louisa M. R. Stead (1850–1917)

LOUISA STEAD and her husband were relaxing with their four-year-old daughter on a Long Island beach when they heard a desperate child's cry. A boy was drowning, and Louisa's husband tried to rescue him. In the process, however, the boy pulled Mr. Stead under the water, and both drowned as Louisa and her daughter watched.

Louisa Stead was left with no means of support except the Lord. She and her daughter experienced dire poverty. One morning, when she had neither funds nor food for the day, she opened the front door and found that someone had left food and money on her doorstep. That day she wrote this hymn.

"Trust in God, AND TRUST also in me."
JOHN 14:1

To God Be the Glory

To God be the glory—great things He hath done!
So loved He the world that He gave us His Son,
Who yielded His life an atonement for sin,
And opened the life-gate that all may go in.

Praise the Lord, praise the Lord,
Let the earth hear His voice!
Praise the Lord, praise the Lord,
Let the people rejoice!
O come to the Father through Jesus the Son,
And give Him the glory—great things He hath done!

Great things He hath taught us, great things He hath done,
And great our rejoicing through Jesus the Son;
But purer, and higher, and greater will be
Our wonder, our transport, when Jesus we see.

FANNY JANE CROSBY (1820–1915)

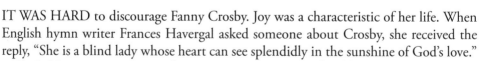

IT WAS HARD to discourage Fanny Crosby. Joy was a characteristic of her life. When English hymn writer Frances Havergal asked someone about Crosby, she received the reply, "She is a blind lady whose heart can see splendidly in the sunshine of God's love."

Probably written in 1872, this song was taken to England by Ira Sankey, who led the singing for D. L. Moody's evangelistic campaigns. The hymn became immediately popular in England, but was published in only a few American hymnals until Billy Graham rediscovered the song during his 1952 British crusade. It then became as popular in America as it had been in England.

Great is the LORD!
He is most worthy
of praise!
Psalm 145:3

TRUST AND OBEY

When we walk with the Lord in the light of His Word,
What a glory He sheds on our way!
While we do His good will He abides with us still,
And with all who will trust and obey.

Trust and obey, for there's no other way
To be happy in Jesus, but to trust and obey.

Then in fellowship sweet we will sit at His feet,
Or we'll walk by His side in the way;
What He says we will do, where He sends we will go—
Never fear, only trust and obey.

JOHN H. SAMMIS (1846–1919)

THIS SONG was written after a D. L. Moody evangelistic meeting in Brockton, Massachusetts. Daniel Towner was the song leader that night in 1886, and he asked the people to share how they had been saved. Several stood and spoke of how certain they felt of their salvation. But then a young man rose and said, "I am not quite sure, but I am going to trust, and I am going to obey."

Towner couldn't forget that testimony. He jotted it down and sent it to John Sammis, who had recently left a career in business to enter the ministry, with the hope that Sammis would find in it the inspiration for a hymn text. Towner was not disappointed.

Under His Wings I Am Safely Abiding

Under His wings I am safely abiding;
Though the night deepens and tempests are wild,
Still I can trust Him—I know He will keep me;
He has redeemed me and I am His child.

Under His wings, under His wings,
Who from His love can sever?
Under His wings my soul shall abide,
Safely abide forever.

Under His wings, O what precious enjoyment!
There will I hide till life's trials are o'er;
Sheltered, protected, no evil can harm me;
Resting in Jesus I'm safe evermore.

WILLIAM ORCUTT CUSHING (1823–1902)

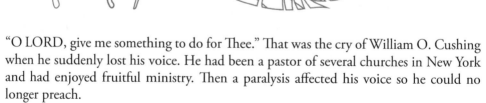

"O LORD, give me something to do for Thee." That was the cry of William O. Cushing when he suddenly lost his voice. He had been a pastor of several churches in New York and had enjoyed fruitful ministry. Then a paralysis affected his voice so he could no longer preach.

Not yet fifty years old, Cushing wondered how God could possibly use him. But God did. Cushing wrote texts for more than three hundred hymns and gospel songs and teamed up with some of the best-known gospel composers of the day.

When he was seventy-three, this prolific hymn writer was moved by the words of Psalm 17:8, "Hide me in the shadow of your wings," and thought about God's care for him even when everything seemed dark. This song was the result.

WE GATHER TOGETHER

May God be merciful and bless us. May his face smile with favor on us. May your ways be known throughout the earth, your saving power among people everywhere.

Psalm 67:1-2

We gather together to ask the Lord's blessing;
He chastens and hastens His will to make known;
The wicked oppressing now cease from distressing,
Sing praises to His name: He forgets not His own.

Beside us to guide us, our God with us joining,
Ordaining, maintaining His kingdom divine;
So from the beginning the fight we were winning:
Thou, Lord, wast at our side, all glory be Thine!

We all do extol Thee, Thou Leader triumphant,
And pray that Thou still our Defender wilt be.
Let Thy congregation escape tribulation:
Thy name be ever praised! O Lord, make us free!

NETHERLANDS FOLK HYMN
TRANSLATED BY THEODORE BAKER (1851–1934)

NO ONE KNOWS who the author of this hymn was, but we can trace it to the Netherlands in the first quarter of the seventeenth century. The Dutch were praying for freedom from Spanish oppression.

This hymn was written to give thanks for the victory that was almost in sight. For these Dutch believers, "the wicked oppressing" were the Spaniards, who would "now cease from distressing." And there was no doubt that God should receive the glory for the victory.

Life is often like that. The victory may still be around the corner, but that should not keep us from giving thanks. For Holland, a golden age of prosperity—of world exploration, of artists like Rembrandt and scientists like Leeuwenhoek—was only a few decades away. And blessings like these are merely a foretaste of what God has for us in the future.

208

WERE YOU THERE?

Were you there when they crucified my Lord?
Were you there when they crucified my Lord?
O! Sometimes it causes me to tremble, tremble, tremble!
Were you there when they crucified my Lord?

Were you there when they nailed Him to the tree?
Were you there when they nailed Him to the tree?
O! Sometimes it causes me to tremble, tremble, tremble!
Were you there when they nailed Him to the tree?

Were you there when they laid Him in the tomb?
Were you there when they laid Him in the tomb?
O! Sometimes it causes me to tremble, tremble, tremble!
Were you there when they laid Him in the tomb?

Were you there when He rose up from the dead?
Were you there when He rose up from the dead?
O! Sometimes I feel like shouting glory, glory, glory!
Were you there when He rose up from the dead?

TRADITIONAL SPIRITUAL

THIS FAVORITE HYMN comes from the rich American spiritual tradition, probably developed in the early 1800s by African American slaves. As in most spirituals, the words are simple, seizing on one central theme or concept.

Spirituals tend to have a lot of emotional appeal. As a result, this hymn, like few others, puts the singer *there*. We experience the "tremble" as we sing it. And in the triumphant final stanza, we experience the glory of a risen Lord.

Were you there
when they
crucified
my Lord?

What a Friend We Have in Jesus

Don't worry about anything; instead, pray about everything. Tell God what you need, and thank him for all he has done. Then you will experience God's peace, which exceeds anything we can understand. His peace will guard your hearts and minds as you live in Christ Jesus.

Philippians 4:6-7

What a Friend we have in Jesus,
All our sins and griefs to bear!
What a privilege to carry
Everything to God in prayer!
O what peace we often forfeit,
O what needless pain we bear,
All because we do not carry
Everything to God in prayer!

Are we weak and heavy-laden,
Cumbered with a load of care?
Precious Savior, still our refuge—
Take it to the Lord in prayer.
Do thy friends despise, forsake thee?
Take it to the Lord in prayer;
In His arms He'll take and shield thee,
Thou wilt find a solace there.

JOSEPH MEDLICOTT SCRIVEN (1819–1886)

NOT FAR FROM Port Hope, Ontario, stands a monument with this inscription: "Four miles north, in Pengally's Cemetery, lies the philanthropist and author of this great masterpiece, written at Port Hope, 1857." Above the inscription are the words of this beloved hymn. Joseph Scriven, its author, was a man who had experienced the friendship of Jesus through a life filled with personal tragedy.

Scriven never intended to publish this hymn. He wrote the words to accompany a letter to his mother, who was ill in far-off Ireland. He had no material resources to send her—only a reminder that the most perfect of friends, Jesus Himself, was nearby.

HIS PEACE
WILL GUARD
YOUR HEARTS
AND MINDS
AS YOU LIVE
IN CHRIST JESUS.
PHILIPPIANS 4:7

What Wondrous Love Is This?

Christ has rescued us from the curse pronounced by the law. When he was hung on the cross, he took upon himself the curse for our wrongdoing. For it is written in the Scriptures, "Cursed is everyone who is hung on a tree."

Galatians 3:13

What wondrous love is this, O my soul, O my soul,
What wondrous love is this, O my soul!
What wondrous love is this that caused the Lord of bliss
To bear the dreadful curse for my soul, for my soul,
To bear the dreadful curse for my soul?

What wondrous love is this, O my soul, O my soul,
What wondrous love is this, O my soul!
What wondrous love is this that caused the Lord of life
To lay aside His crown for my soul, for my soul,
To lay aside His crown for my soul?

AMERICAN FOLK HYMN

THIS HYMN has always been associated with the Appalachian area. Like most spirituals, it has been passed down through the generations and exists in several different versions. The melody, based on a six-tone scale, sounds minor to modern ears and has a haunting effect. The text adds to the effect. This is the question of the ages, and after all the glorious celebration of the Easter season, the question remains. What made Him do it? What made Him do it for me?

Christ "bore the dreadful curse" for our soul, and we can ponder that for the rest of our lives. We can also resolve to devote our lives to Him, to please Him, and praise Him through all eternity.

Christ has RESCUED US from the curse PRONOUNCED BY THE LAW.

GALATIANS 3:13

When I Survey the Wondrous Cross

When I survey the wondrous cross
On which the Prince of glory died,
My richest gain I count but loss,
And pour contempt on all my pride.

Forbid it, Lord, that I should boast,
Save in the death of Christ, my God;
All the vain things that charm me most—
I sacrifice them to His blood.

See, from His head, His hands, His feet,
Sorrow and love flow mingled down;
Did e'er such love and sorrow meet,
Or thorns compose so rich a crown?

Were the whole realm of nature mine,
That were a present far too small:
Love so amazing, so divine,
Demands my soul, my life, my all.

Isaac Watts (1674–1748)

FEW BELIEVERS ever learn to truly love the cross of Christ. For though it offers great deliverance, it also demands great sacrifice. Isaac Watts drives this truth home through the words and music of this powerful hymn. Watts was deeply disappointed with the hymns of his day, which failed to inspire his parishioners to genuine worship and holy living. His dissatisfaction led him to compose more than six hundred hymns, all designed to call his congregation to a deeper knowledge and worship of God. This hymn was written in 1707 for use in a Communion service.

The music of this hymn was borrowed from Gregorian chant. Its rich, grave tones call those who sing it to realize the seriousness of Christ's sacrificial death.

AS FOR ME, MAY I NEVER boast about anything EXCEPT THE CROSS of our Lord JESUS CHRIST.
GALATIANS 6:14

When Morning Gilds the Skies

So whether you eat or drink, or whatever you do, do it all for the glory of God. Don't give offense to Jews or Gentiles or the church of God. I, too, try to please everyone in everything I do. I don't just do what is best for me; I do what is best for others so that many may be saved. And you should imitate me, just as I imitate Christ.

1 Corinthians 10:31–11:1

When morning gilds the skies,
My heart awaking cries,
May Jesus Christ be praised!
Alike at work and prayer,
To Jesus I repair;
May Jesus Christ be praised!

The night becomes as day,
When from the heart we say,
May Jesus Christ be praised!
The powers of darkness fear,
When this sweet chant they hear,
May Jesus Christ be praised!

Ye nations of mankind,
In this your concord find,
May Jesus Christ be praised!
Let all the earth around
Ring joyous with the sound,
May Jesus Christ be praised!

GERMAN HYMN (NINETEENTH CENTURY)
STANZAS 1 AND 2 TRANSLATED BY
EDWARD CASWALL (1814–1878)
STANZA 3 TRANSLATED BY
ROBERT SEYMOUR BRIDGES (1844–1930)

AN ANONYMOUS German author wrote this hymn, which was first printed in *Katholisches Gesangbuch* of Würtzburg in 1828.

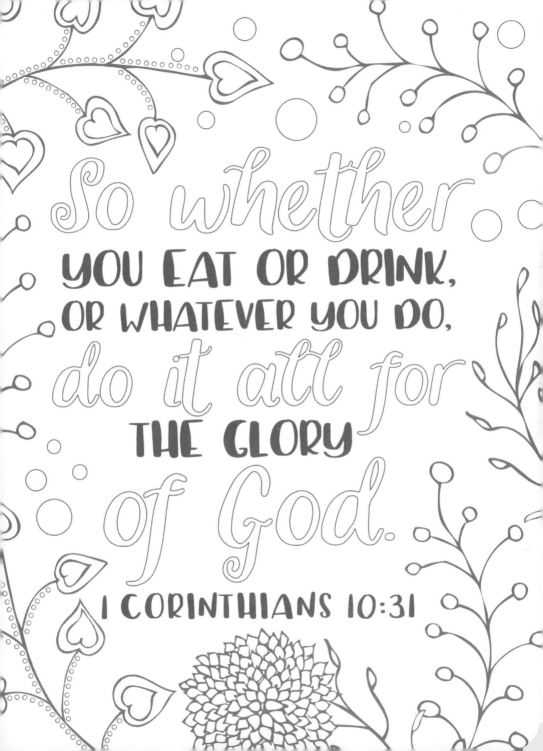

So whether YOU EAT OR DRINK, OR WHATEVER YOU DO, do it all for THE GLORY of God.

1 CORINTHIANS 10:31

Who Is on the Lord's Side?

At this point many of his disciples turned away and deserted him. Then Jesus turned to the Twelve and asked, "Are you also going to leave?" Simon Peter replied, "Lord, to whom would we go? You have the words that give eternal life."

John 6:66-68

Who is on the Lord's side? Who will serve the King?
Who will be His helpers, other lives to bring?
Who will leave the world's side? Who will face the foe?
Who is on the Lord's side? Who for Him will go?
By Thy call of mercy, by Thy grace divine,
We are on the Lord's side, Savior, we are Thine.

Not for weight of glory, not for crown and palm,
Enter we the army, raise the warrior psalm;
But for love that claimeth lives for whom He died;
He whom Jesus nameth must be on His side.
By Thy love constraining, by Thy grace divine,
We are on the Lord's side, Savior, we are Thine.

Fierce may be the conflict, strong may be the foe,
But the King's own army none can overthrow.
Round His standard ranging; vict'ry is secure;
For His truth unchanging makes the triumph sure.
Joyfully enlisting by Thy grace divine,
We are on the Lord's side, Savior, we are Thine.

FRANCES RIDLEY HAVERGAL (1836–1879)

FOR SOMEONE who struggled with illness much of her life, Frances Ridley Havergal wrote a remarkable number of vigorous, robust hymns. The last manuscript she worked on was *Starlight through the Shadows,* a book for invalids. She died before she could complete the book, but her sister added the final chapter from Havergal's unpublished papers. That chapter is entitled "Marching Orders" and concludes with the words of this hymn.

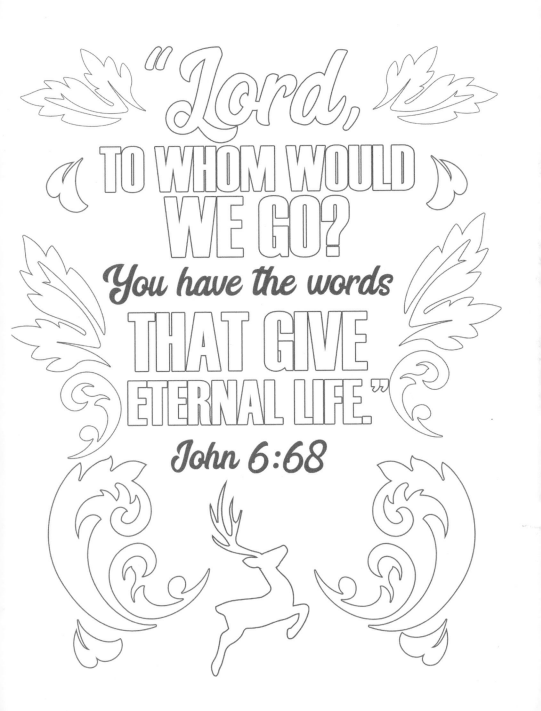

Wonderful Grace of Jesus

Wonderful grace of Jesus,
Greater than all my sin;
How shall my tongue describe it,
Where shall its praise begin?
Taking away my burden,
Setting my spirit free,
For the wonderful grace of Jesus reaches me.

Wonderful the matchless grace of Jesus,
Deeper than the mighty rolling sea;
Higher than the mountain, sparkling like a fountain,
All sufficient grace for even me;
Broader than the scope of my transgressions,
Greater far than all my sin and shame;
O magnify the precious name of Jesus,
Praise His name!

Wonderful grace of Jesus,
Reaching the most defiled,
By its transforming power
Making me God's dear child,
Purchasing peace and heaven
For all eternity—
And the wonderful grace of Jesus reaches me.

HALDOR LILLENAS (1885–1959)

IN 1917, young pastor Haldor Lillenas and his wife were settling into a ministry at the Nazarene church of Auburn, Illinois. After buying a house in nearby Olivet, they had little money left to furnish it. Then Haldor found a "wheezy little organ" in the home of a neighbor and paid five dollars for it. Lillenas wrote a number of songs on that instrument, including this one.

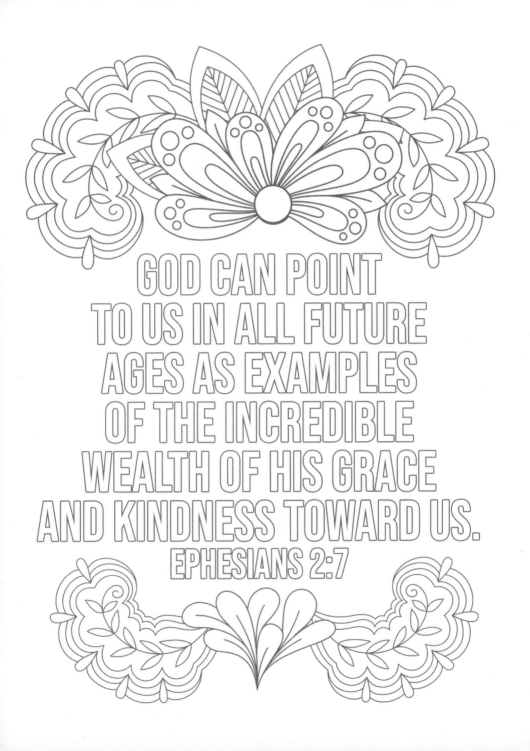

GOD CAN POINT
TO US IN ALL FUTURE
AGES AS EXAMPLES
OF THE INCREDIBLE
WEALTH OF HIS GRACE
AND KINDNESS TOWARD US.
EPHESIANS 2:7

Inspire *The Bible for Coloring & Creative Journaling*

Original Edition

Hardcover LeatherLike	Large Print LeatherLike
978-1-4964-1374-1	978-1-4964-1986-6

Praise Edition

LeatherLike	Large Print HC
978-1-4964-2984-1	LeatherLike
	978-1-4964-3346-6

Prayer Edition

LeatherLike	Giant Print LeatherLike
978-1-4964-2409-9	978-1-4964-5497-3

Girls Edition

Softcover	HC LeatherLike	LeatherLike
978-1-4964-2661-1	978-1-4964-2665-9	978-1-4964-5495-9

Catholic Bible

HC LeatherLike	Large Print	LeatherLike
978-1-4964-3657-3	LeatherLike	978-1-4964-5496-6
	978-1-4964-4683-1	

Coloring–Book Style

Inspire: Psalms	Inspire: Proverbs	Inspire: Matthew & Mark	Inspire: Luke & John	Inspire: Acts & Romans	Inspire: 1 Cor—2 Thes	Inspire: 1 Tim—
978-1-4964-1987-3	978-1-4964-2664-2	978-1-4964-5498-0	978-1-4964-5499-7	978-1-4964-5500-0	978-1-4964-5501-7	978-1-4964-550